IMPROVE YOUR ENGLISH

By
Dr. B. JAMES

GOODWILL PUBLISHING HOUSE®
B-3 RATTAN JYOTI, 18 RAJENDRA PLACE
NEW DELHI -110008 (INDIA)

© Publishers

All rights reserved. No part of this publication may be reproduced; stored in a retrieval system or transmitted in any form or by any means, mechanical, photocopying or otherwise without the prior written permission of the publisher.

Published by
GOODWILL PUBLISHING HOUSE®
B-3 Rattan Jyoti, 18 Rajendra Place
New Delhi-110008 (INDIA)
Tel. : 25750801, 25820556
Fax : 91-11-25764396
E-mail : goodwillpub@vsnl.net
website : www.goodwillpublishinghouse.com

Printed at
Rajiv Book Binding House, Delhi

Contents

1. How to Improve Your English 1
2. Sentence Formation 11
3. Discipline of Writing 21
4. Correct Use of Parts of Speech 32
5. Bricks that Build 70
6. How to Improve Your Writing Power-1 135
7. How to Improve Your Writing Power-2 140
8. How to Improve Your Writing Power-3 147
9. How to Improve Your Writing Power-4 156
10. How to Increase Your Speaking Power-1 169
11. How to Increase Your Speaking Power-2 180

1
How to Improve Your English

Introduction

Language is more than a medium of communication. It reflects your cultural background, it reveals your personality and it organises your thoughts. It is with the help of language that we can convince others and compel them to believe what we believe in. That is why, whether you are taking an examination or you are writing a letter or an article or you are discussing with your friends or you are at an interview, you need impressive and highly communicative language. It was the thunderous speech of Sir Winston Churchill that made the Germans commit the folly of attacking Russia instead of attacking England during the Second World War. It was the emotional and cautiously-worded speech of Antony, in Shakespeare's *Julius Caesar* that made him popular and down-grade Brutus. What wonders carefully-worded speeches can work!

You cannot be born with a mastery over the language; you have to acquire it with persistent labour. If you have an aptitude for it, you can acquire it more quickly. But you cannot reach the end point at any stage; improving language is a continuous process.

There are many hurdles in the way of a learner. We depend more on journalistic writings—newspapers, magazines etc.—

for our knowledge of the language. We forget that language used in journalistic writings is not standard English. You may call it "functional English". For example in the newspapers you come across the phrase "family members" but in standard English, it should be "members of the family." Similarly, in journalistic idiom, it is correct to say : "they were asked to quickly decide" but in standard English it is an incorrect sentence because there is split infinitive in it. The sentence should be "They were asked to decide quickly."

Another obstacle is that it is a foreign language, so the sentence construction differs from the sentence patterns in Indian languages. So, if we do not learn English right from our childhood, we do not become familiar with the turns and twists of the language. Moreover, we think in Indian languages and try to express in English. Thus, unconsciously we translate our thoughts into English but such a translation does not convey the spirit. One cannot learn a language through translation. Tagore, in this context says, "you cannot woo a lady through an attorney." It is also said that languages are jealous among themselves and do not yield their treasure to other languages.

Teaching of English at the early stages of schooling is way below the mark. Teaching is more or less a mechanical process at these stages. Whether it is "play-way method" or "visual perception method", teachers fail to excite the interest of the children. If at all they take interest, it is because the language is new to them and their parents are very happy when their children speak a few words of English. But this interest does not last long. Moreover, at home they talk in their mother tongue.

Another obstacle in our effort to learn English is our inability to buy standard English books and read them. At school stage, if at all we read, we read comics or detective novels which in no way help us in improving our language or expression.

Keeping the above mentioned hurdles and problems in mind, we will have to devise some methods of adopting effective methods for improving English.

Reading, Speaking, Writing

For learning a language reading, speaking and writing should go together. Reading enriches our knowledge which in its turn serves as a spur to original thinking. Speaking organises the thoughts in their logical sequence; this helps in the continuous flow of ideas and the mind becomes quick in selecting words. Writing makes the language scientific, accurate and effective.

Reading. Which books should we read? In fact, we should read prose writings of well-known English writers of today. Prose writings of B. Russell, A.L. Huxley, G.B. Shaw, Nirad C. Chaudhri, Naipaul etc. should be read. Magazines and newspapers cannot help us much. Just going through the book is not enough. Read one paragraph and cull out the main ideas and arguments. Try to put these ideas in your own way. Then compare the two — the one which you have written and the other written by the writer. Discover your weaknesses —

(a) Whether you are unable to select proper words (b) if you have failed to explain the idea in a proper manner (c) if

you have failed to make the whole description effective. When you write again, try to remove these defects.

While going through the book, collect impressive phrases and note them down in a note book. Revise them from time to time so that you may commit them to memory. When you come to writing, make use of them. In this manner, these phrases will become a part of your thinking and will not import any discrepancy in your style.

Speaking. If you have not been conversing in English with the members of your family and friends, you will experience a lot of difficulty in speaking. So better begin reading a few paragraphs from a book loudly and as fast as you can. When you feel that your reading is very smooth, come to the next step. Start speaking loudly on simple topics that you know. For example, you may speak on "Members of my family," "My School days" or "Train journey" etc. Then you can come to more argumentative and difficult topics if you feel that you can speak well on simple topics. Your emphasis should be on the flow of the language in the initial stages. Then you should try to make your language free from mistakes. It will be good if you use a tape recorder, for then you will be able to evaluate your speech. You should also see if your speech has developed logically and ideas cohere themselves with one another.

Writing. Writing is as important as reading and speaking. Just writing for the sake of writing is not enough. You will have to make a sincere and conscious effort to write better.

Begin writing on simple topics but your approach should be fresh. There should be touches of imagination here and there. For example, the idea "We have made economic progress but this is not enough" has been put thus by a writer :

> While there has been substantial economic recovery but we are not out of the shadows yet and there is no room for complacency.

Some lay stress on a particular point with the help of various methods—rhetorical language, details and ramifications contributing to the main idea and weaving patterns like a magician who throws balls of different colours into the air and then catches them. Read a paragraph from the speech of Mr. Churchill and discover its beauty:

> Freedom will be erected on unshakable foundations and at her side will be Right and Justice and I am sure of this that when victory is gained, we shall show a poise and temper as admirable as that which we displayed in the days of our mortal danger that we shall not be led astray by false guides either into apathy and weakness or into brutality but that the name of our dear country, our island home will be our conduct by our clairvoyance, by our self restraint,

by our inflexible tenacity of purpose long stand in honour amongst the nations of the world!

So write once, then try to improve it. Thus, you will be training your intellectual processes for better expression. With practice, you will find a style suitable to your personality and thinking.

Improve Your Thinking Process

Language is coloured by one's thinking process. Those who are simple-minded and think straight, will always be simple and straightforward in their language. Read the following paragraph from Gandhiji's writings and you will find it simple and straightforward :

Exploitation of the poor can be extinguished not by effecting the destruction of a few millionaires but by removing the ignorance of the poor and teaching them not to co-operate with their exploiters. That will convert the exploiters also. I have even suggested that ultimately, it will lead to both being equal partners.

In the above quoted paragraph, ideas flow in an effortless manner and they have a logical relation; there is a chain of thoughts. Some people are not clear in their thoughts, so their language is involved and complex and they labour to explain their ideas. For example :

Effective rational propaganda becomes possible only when there is a clear understanding, on the part of all concerned, of the nature of symbols and of their relation to the things and events symbolised. Irrational propaganda depends for its effectiveness on a general failure to understand the nature of symbols. Simple-minded people tend to equate the symbol with what it stands for, to attribute to things and events some of the qualities expressed by the words in terms of which the propagandist has chosen for his own purposes, to talk about them.

In the above quoted paragraph, so many modifying ideas are given in each sentence that the attention of the reader cannot be fixed on one point This is not because the thinking is ambiguous but because the related ideas appear so fast in mind that one is forced to pack them together. The writer wants to give a very comprehensive explanation of an idea in a single sentence. Such writing poses a great problem to the reader.

All great writers, who are famous for their effective style, are simple, to the point and straightforward. For example Nirad C. Chaudhri is known for his effective style; read the following lines by him, about Oxford—

> *The university was still a club — a religious, scholarly and epicurean club for its teaching members, a recreational, sporting and talking club for its student members, and a social club for both.*

It is a fine imaginative presentation of a simple idea.

Now the question arises, How to cultivate our thinking process ? Firstly, we should think in English before writing. As has been pointed out earlier, if we think in Hindi and write in English, we translate the idea in our sub-conscious mind and this can never be accurate. For this, we will have to make maximum use of English, while speaking or writing. Secondly, we should develop the habit of thinking straight. Think over a topic in a logical manner. If the topic demands arguments, think 'how', 'why', 'what' of the topic. If it is narrative, think of the chronology of events. Without thinking straight, your language cannot be simple and straightforward. Thirdly, straight thinking also depends on vocabulary. If you have a good vocabulary at your command, words will help you to think properly. If you do not have a good vocabulary, you have to fumble for words and you think of putting the idea in a different manner. The presentation thus becomes involved.

Personality Influences Thinking

It may sound strange but is a fact that the personality of the writer colours his thinking and writing. Great writers do not grow like a mushroom on a dung hill; these have to be cultivated like roses in the garden. A good writer will have to develop a healthy moral, mental and material outlook towards life. If a person is not endowed with a suitable personality, one has to cultivate it. A good writer will have to be (i) a good observer of man and affairs of men (ii) analytical in approach (iii) comprehensive in thinking (iv) sensitive to impressions (v) desirous to correlate information. It is this part of the personality that can be called intellectual make-up, which influences thinking and so also writing and speaking.

If a person cannot observe life closely, and minutely, he cannot have material for writing or illustrating. Sherlock Holmes, the hero of the detective novels of Conan Doyle could derive much information even from a hat lying on a dunghill. So should be a writer. Life gives us material for writing. A writer must have a knowledge of the social, cultural and economic life of the people. Even when you are a student, you need this knowledge because this can provide you much stuff for writing and speaking. You can illustrate your point, you can substantiate your argument and you can come close to reality. If keen observation is supplemented with the reading of good books, the knowledge becomes more comprehensive. By contrasting and comparing your knowledge with the knowledge of other writers, one becomes more scientific in knowledge.

A speaker or a writer must have a talent to analyse the situation, correlate it with other information and then come to generalisation. This intellectual approach will organise his thoughts and help him to express them. He will not have to wait for the ideas.

A person who is not comprehensive in thinking cannot be persuasive in speech or writing. If all the aspects of the problem are addressed, it leaves no scope for the reader to doubt its validity. No letter, no agreement, no article can appeal to the reader unless it is quite comprehensive. You can speak for a longer time and write in detail if you study all the aspects of the problem. One-sided view comes limping to the reader and so does not sink into his mind. An isolated incident or a piece of information does not appeal to the reader but when it is given a wider context and related to other aspects, it has an appeal. For example, if I say that "Mr. A is bad because he is a politician", people may consider it a prejudiced opinion. But if I give details of his actions and talk about more politicians in that very vein i.e. make 't more comprehensive, the readers will be persuaded to believe.

Comprehensiveness also provides variety to a piece of writing. A writer with a limited vision cannot talk about variety of things. But we should not forget that variety is the spice of life. It broadens our outlook and enriches our mind. If our brain is a mine of information, we can overawe the reader by the sheer wealth of information. We make the reader or the listener our intellectual disciple.

No speaker or writer can make a mark unless he is sensitive to impressions. The same incidents or happenings arouse different types of reaction in the case of different people. The song of the nightingale made Keats to sing—

Fade far away, dissolve, and quite forget
What thou among the leave last never known,
The weariness, the fever, and the fret
Here, where men sit and hear each other groan;
Where palsy shakes a few, sad, last gray hairs,
Where youth grows pale, and spectle-thin, and dies;
Where but to think is to be full of sorrow
And leaden-eyed despairs;
Where Beauty cannot keep her lustrous eyes,
Or now love pine at them beyond tomorrow.

It is a vivid picture of the miseries of life and seems to be remotely connected with the song of the nightingale. But a person sensitive to impressions often finds that the whole gamut of emotions is touched by a single incident and his kaleidoscopic imagination weaves different patterns out of it. Clearly, a person sensitive to impressions, retains much in his mind, certain words, or ideas become associated with happenings.

Correlating information is possible if one is sensitive to impressions and comprehensive in thinking. If a person cannot establish relation, whether imaginary or real, he can not improve his thinking and expression. For consolidating his ideas and opinions, this correlation is essential. Correlating information does not mean just putting information together, it means to discover their similarity, contrast, or an other type of relationship. This adds many arrows to one's quiver. The larger the number of pieces of information, the greater will be your search for words to express them. The richer the thoughts, the richer will be the language. Ideas do not die due to their excessive weight; they create a strong craving for expression. It is an over-whelming emotion like anger or love which must find an outlet. Language automatically becomes better.

Concluding Remarks

From this discussion one can gather that English cannot be improved by simply reading books or by simply increasing vocabulary. It requires an all-out effort to make it more effective. The whole personality will have to be coloured by it. If you read English books, converse in English and write in English, you start thinking in English.

All this should be supplemented with a conscious effort to make your language better. Think if you can use a better phrase than the one which is used by you. You can pick up good phrases from standard writers and remember them. Make use of them while writing. The phrases will become a part of your thinking and your language, as well as presentation, will improve.

Before adopting methods for improvement, one should fix one's aim — whether improvement is to be made for writing effectively or for speaking effectively. In either case, we will have to adopt a little different technique. The following chapter will make it clear that the language for effective speaking is different from that of effective writing.

➢➢➢

2
Sentence Formation

A word gives a unit of thought whereas a sentence is a unit of an argument or a paragraph. The Oxford dictionary defines a sentence thus : "a number of words making a grammatically complete structure generally begun with a capital letter and ends with a full stop or its equivalent." Clearly, words go into the making of a sentence. But words must be arranged in a particular manner. This is called syntax in grammar.

Parts of Speech

Words used in a sentence serve one or the other grammatical functions. In other words, it may be used as a subject (i.e. doer) or as a verb (act of doing) etc. These grammatical functions are called parts of speech. In English language, following are the parts of speech.

Noun. Which is either subject or object e.g. "John meets Baker". Both 'John' and 'Baker' are nouns.

Verb. Which may be transitive or intransitive e.g. "He works hard." The word 'works' is a verb.

Adjective. Words which qualify a noun e.g. "Ram is a good boy.' The word 'good' is an adjective.

Pronoun. A word used in place of a noun e.g. he, she, it etc.

Adverb. Words which qualify a verb e.g. "He has come late." The word "late" is an adverb.

Conjunction. Words which join two parts of a sentence. e.g. "He has committed murder so he will be punished." The word "so" is the conjunction.

Preposition. Preposition is a word placed before a noun or noun-equivalent to show in what relation the person or thing denoted by the noun stands to something else. e.g. "I said to him." The word 'to' is the preposition.

Interjection. Interjection is a word or sound thrown into a sentence to express some feeling of mind. e.g. "Alas! he has failed". The word "alas" is the interjection.

Articles. Articles do not constitute any distinct part of speech; these are adjectives in their functions e.g. 'a', 'an', 'the'.

Participle. It is a double part of speech i.e. verb and adjective. These are the two functions it can perform. These are of two types — Present participle and Past participle. e.g.

1. It is a disappointing situation.
2. He is leaving today.
3. She is a trained technician.
4. He laughed at him.

"Disappointing" in sentence 1 is an adjective. "Leaving" in sentence 2 is also a present participle used as subject. 'Trained' in sentence 3 is past participle used as an adjective. "Laughed" in sentence 4 is past participle used as a verb.

Gerund is a verbal noun i.e. a noun formed with a verb e.g. "Parking is prohibited." Parking is used as a noun (subject) so it is a gerund.

Infinitive is just a verb with 'to' or without 'to'.

We will study the correct use of these parts of speech in the following chapter. Here we will be concerned with the placement of these parts of speech in different types of sentences.

Types of Sentences

There are five types of sentences :
(1) Assertive

SENTENCE FORMATION

(2) Interrogative
(3) Imperative
(4) Exclamatory
(5) Optative.

Assertive. A sentence which just makes a statement, e.g. This house is vacant. It can be affirmative or negative.

Interrogative. A sentence which asks a question, e.g. What do you want?

Imperative. A sentence which makes a request, advice or order, e.g. Run away.

Exclamatory sentences are those which express a feeling of pleasure, disgust, pity, surprise etc., e.g. What a fine idea!

Optative. A sentence which expresses a wish, e.g. May you live long!

Mechanics of Sentence Formation

While framing a sentence we name or speak about a person or a thing and say or predicate something about that person or thing. The naming part is called SUBJECT and saying part is PREDICATE. Every sentence must have these two parts i.e. subject and predicate. The subject and predicate may consist of one word or several words.

The nucleus of the subject i.e. the most important word in the whole subject is called *subject-word or subject.* The nucleus of the predicate is *predicate word or finite verb.* It is a round these words that the whole sentence is built up.

In *assertive sentences* the subject is generally placed before the finite verb. *For example :*

He has bought the book.

'He' is the subject and 'has bought' is the verb. But sometimes for the sake of emphasis the verb may be put before the noun. *For example :*

Up went the flag.

In *interrogative sentences* the finite verb or auxiliary verb is put before the noun or pronoun. *For example :*

Has he finished the work?
Do you know him?
Why do you not speak?

In all these sentences the verb is put before the subject.

In **imperative sentences** the subject is generally omitted. *For example :*

Leave this place.
Speak out the whole thing.

In **exclamatory sentences**, though the normal position of the subject is after the finite verb but many a time it is left out. *For example :*

How glamorous!
How amazing is the spirit of man!

Rules Regarding Sentence Formation

For composing a good sentence we must know the art of arranging words, clauses and phrases in a sentence. It is with the help of this arrangement that we can make our sentences smooth and effective. But we cannot put words, phrases and clauses in any pattern we like; some rules will have to be observed.

Rule of Proximity

It means that things which are to be thought of together must be mentioned together. It also holds good for the position of qualifying words, phrases and clauses. *For example :*

 1. *Wanted a nurse for an infant of 20 years*

The above given sentence violates the rule of proximity. The sentence means that the infant is of 20 years but an infant is a baby in arms and cannot be of 20 years. So in the corrected sentence 'of 20 years' should be placed immediately after 'nurse', because it refers to the 'nurse'.

SENTENCE FORMATION

  2. *He visited the place where Lord Krishna delivered his message during his holidays.*

The sentence as it is, means that Lord Krishna was having holidays when he delivered the message. So this phrase is connected with 'visited' and not with 'delivered' so the phrase should be put in the beginning of the sentence.

  3. *All except him had left the place so only I spoke to him.*

In the above given sentence, the word *only* qualifies the pronoun 'I' so it means "none else but I" whereas, the sentence demands that *"Only"* should qualify him. So the correct latter part of the sentence is — 'I spoke to him only.'

Rule of Priority

According to this rule, qualifying phrases and clauses should, as far as idiom or the context allows, precede the clause or words to which they are subordinate. *For example :*

  I realised as I took the decision that I was the loser.

In the above given sentence, the clause "as I took the decision" is subordinate to "I realised" so the former should precede the latter. The corrected sentence is —

  As I took the decision I realised that I was the loser.

Another example is —

  I had forgotten when he came to me what he had said.

The corrected sentence is —

  When he came to me I had forgotten what he had said.

The principle underlying this rule is that the reader is kept in suspense. His interest is aroused to know what is coming and when it comes it comes with great force. Thus the principal clause receives the emphasis it was supposed to receive. But the rule of priority has to be sacrificed for the sake of clarity or for one or the other demand, of the context.

Rule of Consistency

There should be consistency in the different parts of a sentence. Unrelated thoughts in a sentence makes it not only grammatically incorrect but also thematically ridiculous. *For example*

We had been praying and the judge did not listen.

His father suffered a heart attack and his mother had heart attack.

The king died and the queen died.

The two parts of the *first* sentence have no thematic relation. The second clause just gives additional information but the wording of the first clause demands that the second should complete the idea. So we should replace **and** by **but**.

In the *second sentence,* two pieces of information are given but both are not related. If we rewrite the sentence thus. "His father suffered a heart attack, so did his mother." It becomes connected.

The *third sentence* is also with unrelated thoughts. The two incidents — the king's death and the queen's death — are unrelated. But the sentence develops consistency if we say : "The king died **because** the queen died."

Consistency is essential not only for making the sentence readable but also for making it an effective link in the chain of ideas. If one idea leads to the other and that to the next, the thought-process absorbs the whole easily.

Logicality of sentences. Allied to consistency is the logical sequence of ideas. Sometimes a part of a sentence contradicts the other part of the sentence and so the sentence becomes incorrect. *For example :*

Stretch this barbed wire between each pole.

The sentence is illogical. Nothing can be stretched between each pole. We can stretch a wire only between two poles. So

SENTENCE FORMATION

the word **each** should be replaced by **two**. Another example is —

> When this child first saw day light it was born without eyes.

No person without eyes can see daylight though "first saw day light" is an idiom and means "born"; still it should agree with the later part even in its literal sense. So the idiom should be replaced by 'born.'

What should be the length of a sentence?

No doubt the length of a sentence depends upon the number of ideas we want to pack up in a sentence. But it should be neither too long nor too short. Long sentences scatter the attention of the reader, whereas, short sentences may make our mind skip over it. So a sentence should be of moderate length.

A sentence with a number of clauses will never be able to rivet our attention, rather it will confuse the reader. Sometimes we fail to connect the subject with the verb. *For example :*

> An intelligent reader who buys good books which are written by foreign writers and which are published by Indian publishers enjoying world wide reputation which they have earned with honest labour, is rare.

In the above given sentence there are so many adjectival clauses qualifying the nouns. The clause "who buys good books" qualifies reader, "which... are writers" qualifies books, "which are... publishers" also qualifies books and so on. The subject "intelligent reader" is to be connected with the verb i.e. "is rare". The sentence has become confusing.

Short sentences are used for (i) effectiveness (ii) pin pointing an idea (iii) expressing strong emotions. After discussing a point with the help of illustrations, similes and such like, tricks of writing a short sentence comes like the fall of the hammer. It not only focusses our attention but drives the point home. A short sentence can be easily managed by the writer. There is no distraction by the clauses. So if we want to pin point a particular idea we write a short sentence. But if all the sentences are short, the purpose of writing a short sentence is frustrated. Thirdly, strong emotions are best expressed with the help of a short sentence. As emotion, choke a person, he can not speak many words and so the sentences are short.

Examples of sentence formation :

(A) Forming Simple Sentences by Combining Two

(i) By using a participle. *Example :*
   I heard the noise. I rushed to the place.
   Simple : *On hearing the noise I rushed to the place.*

(ii) By using a preposition with a gerund. *Example :*
   He caught fish. In this way he made a living.
   Simple : *He caught fish for making a living.*

(iii) By using an infinitive. *For example :*
   I have no money. I cannot pay the bill.
   Simple: *I have no money to pay the bill.*

(iv) Buy using a noun or a noun-phrase in apposition. *Example :*
   Lord Clive founded the British Empire. He was a clerk in the company.
   Simple : *Lord Clive, the founder of the British Empire was a clerk in the company.*

(v) By using an adverb or adverbial phrases. *Example :*
   He won the toss. He was fortunate.
   Simple : *Being fortunate, he won the toss.* Or *Fortunately, he won the toss.*

(B) Formation of Simple Sentences from Complex Sentences

(i) By using a noun for a noun clause :
   Complex : *Tell me where you were born.*
   Simple : *Tell me about your birthplace.*

SENTENCE FORMATION

(ii) By using an adjective or participle :

Complex : *Such candidates as work hard will get through.*

Simple : *Hard-working candidates will get through.*

(iii) By using a noun in the genitive case :

Complex : *They soon forgot the labours they had undergone.*

Simple : *They soon forgot the past labours.*

(iv) By using a preposition with its object :

Complex : *The benefit that he derived from his early training was lost.*

Simple : *The benefit of his early training was lost.*

(v) By using a gerundial infinitive :

Complex : *I have no money that I can spare.*

Simple : *I have no money to spare.*

(vi) By using a compound noun :

Complex : *That is the place where my father was buried.*

Simple : *That is my father's burial place.*

(vii) By using a preposition or prepositional phrases :

Complex : *The boy was pleased that he had won a prize.*

Simple : *The boy was pleased at having won a prize.*

(viii) By using a participle :

Complex : *As the main point has been gained, success is certain.*

Simple : *The main point having being gained, success is certain.*

(ix) By using gerundial infinitive :

Complex : *They were surprised when they heard him.*

Simple : *They were surprised to hear him.*

(C) Formation of Multiple Sentences to Complex

(i) By using cumulative conjunction :

Multiple : *Speak the truth and you need have no fear.*

Complex : *If you speak the truth you need have no fear.*

(ii) By using alternative conjunctions :

Multiple : *Leave this room or I will compel you to do so.*

Complex : *Unless you leave this room I will compel you to do so.*

(iii) By using adversative conjunctions :

Multiple : *He was poor man but he was always honest.*

Complex : *He was always honest although he was poor.*

(iv) By using illative conjunctions :

Multiple : *He was very tired therefore he fell sound asleep*

Complex : *He fell sound asleep because he was tired.*

3

Discipline of Writing

Language is, no doubt, a medium of communication, yet any combination of words cannot be language. Words must be filled in a sentence according to a definite pattern. That pattern for every language is provided by its grammar. Like other languages, English also follows certain rules of grammar. So the knowledge of the rules of correct English is an absolute necessity for improving English.

After going through the list of common errors in English, one may get an impression that it is quite tedious to keep so many rules in mind. But only regular practice can make these rules a part of your thinking. As I pointed out in the first chapter, for improving English one must read, write and speak.

This should be done by keeping the rules in mind. I agree that in conversation or spoken English, complete sentences are rarely spoken. These sentences are not correct in standard written English. Still, the rules concerning the construction of sentences must be studied so that these may not become meaningless.

Common Errors in English

We have already read that there are three important parts of a sentence — Noun, Verb and Predicate. Adjectives, adverbs and adjectival or adverbial phrases or clauses are the other parts of a sentence. Their correct uses are the foundations of good English.

Agreement between Noun and Verb. If a noun or a pronoun is plural in number, the verb should also be plural and if it is singular, the verb should agree with it. But the rule is not so simple in its application as it seems to be. Following are the different aspects of its application.

(a) When two nouns or pronouns are joined by a 'Neither... nor', 'Either... or' "Not only but also" the verb should agree with the second noun or pronoun. *For example :*

1. *Incorrect* : Neither he nor I *is* responsible.
   Correct   : Neither he nor I *am* responsible.
2. *Incorrect* : Either he or his friends *is* ready to make these irresponsible statements.
   Correct   : Either he or his friends *are* ready to make these irresponsible statements.
3. *Incorrect* : Not only the minister but also his party men *is* against me.
   Correct   : Not only the minister but also his party men *are* against me.

(b) When two nouns or pronouns are joined by "as well as" the verb should agree with the first noun or pronoun. *For example :*

Incorrect : He as well as I *am* to attend the meeting.
Correct   : He as well as I is to attend the meeting.

DISCIPLINE OF WRITING

(c) When there are two subjects in the clauses of a sentence, relate them with their actual verbs. *For example:*

Incorrect : He is one of those who *has* been defeated.
Correct   : He is one of those who *have* been defeated.

In the above given sentence *'he'* and *'who'* are the subjects. The latter pronoun refers to *those.* So the verb following it should be plural — *have* and not *has.*

(d) A collective noun (single noun referring to many) when used collectively should take singular verb but if it refers to its members then the verb should be plural.

Incorrect : The hockey team *have* won the match.
Correct   : The hockey team *has* won the match.

In the above given sentence, the team as a whole has won the match. So the noun *'team'* is used collectively.

Incorrect : The teams *has* taken their places in the field.
Correct   : The teams *have* taken their places in the field.

(i) The poet and statesman has passed away.
(ii) The poet and the stateman have passed away.

(e) 'The poet and statesman' refers to one person whereas 'the poet and the statesman' refers to two persons. So the first phrase will take singular verb, whereas, the second will take plural verb. If an article is used with one noun *we* refer to one person and if we use two articles, *we* refer to two persons or things. *Example :*

Incorrect : The manager and secretary of this firm have resigned.
Correct   : The manager and the secretary have resigned.
or
The manager and secretary has resigned.

(f) 'Riches' always means 'wealth' and 'wages' when used in the sense of 'punishment' take singular verb. *Example :*

Incorrect : Riches *have* turned his head.
Correct   : Riches *has* turned his head.

(g) Phrases like "sum and substance," "weal and woe" "bread and butter" take a singular verb because they constitute a single subject. *Example* :

Incorrect : The sum and substance of this poem *are* quite clear.

Correct : The sum and substance of this poem *is* quite clear.

(h) A noun or a pronoun when used as a subject must take a verb which agrees with it. *Example :*

Incorrect : He is one of those who *has been* convicted.

Correct : He is one of those who *have been* convicted.

Correct use of Comparative and Superlative degree

(a) With words which give absolute sense, words with comparative and superlative sense are not used. *Example* :

Incorrect : Make these two lines more parallel.

Correct : Make these lines parallel.

(b) We must compare the same things and not the different ones. *Example :*

Incorrect : Her features are sharper than her mother.

Correct : Her features are shaper than her mother's.

'Feature', must be compared with 'features' but not with 'mother'.

(c) If two degrees of comparison are used in one sentence both should be complete. *Example :*

Incorrect : He is as good if not better than his brother.

Correct : He is as good as if not better than his brother.

Complete positive degree is 'as good as' and complete comparative degree is 'better than.'

(d) Comparative degree when used in the superlative sense, will be followed by 'ANY' when things belong to different

DISCIPLINE OF WRITING

groups and ANY OTHER if they belong to the same group. *Example :*

Incorrect : Kolkata is better than any city in India.

Correct : Kolkata is better than any other city in India.

(e) In modern English, we cannot make use of double comparatives and superlatives. *Example :*

Incorrect : Which course of action is more preferable?

Correct : Which course of action is preferable?

Incorrect : This is perhaps the most best suggestion.

Correct : This is perhaps the best suggestion.

Incorrect : Who is more better — the elder or the younger?

Correct : Who is better — the elder or the younger?

Incorrect : Your friend's performance is more superior to your performance.

Correct : Your friend's performance is superior to your performance.

(f) The words 'junior', 'senior', 'inferior', 'superior' are followed by the preposition 'to' and not by 'than.' *Example :*

Incorrect : Jack is definitely junior than me.

Correct : Jack is definitely junior *to* me.

Incorrect : Those who are senior than you will be promoted.

Correct : Those who are senior *to* you will be promoted.

(g) 'Elder' takes 'to' as preposition whereas 'older' takes 'than'. *Example :*

Incorrect : He is elder than me.

Correct : He is elder *to* me.

Incorrect : This man is older to Elizabeth.

Correct : This man is older *than* Elizabeth.

Placement of Words and Phrases

(a) If a phrase is not put near the word it qualifies, the sentence may give a wrong meaning. Such a sentence will be grammatically incorrect. *For example :*

Incorrect : You wrote that you would meet me in your last letter.

Correct : In your last letter you wrote that you would meet me.

Comments : The incorrect sentence means that you would meet in your last letter. No one can meet in a letter. So the phrase "in your last letter" refers to writing and must be put in the beginning.

Incorrect : This memorial is built in the memory of John who as a *mark of respect* was accidentally shot.

Correct : This memorial is built, as a mark of respect, in the memory of John who was accidentally shot.

Incorrect : Wanted an ailing father *for* a *nurse*.

Correct : Wanted a nurse for an ailing father.

(b) Many a time an adverb is placed at the wrong place and the sentence gives an incorrect meaning. *For example:*

Incorrect : There were so many visitors but the minister only spoke to me.

Correct : There were so many visitors but the minister spoke to me only.

Comments : In the first sentence *only* qualifies "spoke" so it means that he simply spoke and did not do anything else. Where as "me only" means that "I was the only person" with whom he spoke.

(1) I clean this house alone.

(2) I alone I clean this house.

Comments : The first sentence means that the house is cleaned without any one's help. The second means that except me nobody else does it.

(c) Participles (first form of the *verb* + *ing* or third form of the verb) serve as adjectives and *must* be put before the noun they qualify. *For example :*

Incorrect : Departed god may bless the soul.

Correct : God may bless the *departed* soul.

The first sentence means that God has departed whereas "departed" should be used for soul.

Incorrect : I saw a diamond ring walking in the garden.

Correct   : *Walking* in the garden I saw a diamond ring.

Clearly a 'ring' cannot walk so the first sentence is wrong. The second sentence means that "while I was walking in the garden.

Incorrect : *Laughing* he became a stock.

Correct   : He became a *laughing* stock.

Incorrect : He is all the time shop *talking*.

Correct   : He is all the time *talking* shop.

(d) Sometimes a phrase may be put at a place in a sentence that it may be connected with two parts or verbs of the sentence. This will make the sentence ambiguous and so unacceptable in standard English. *For example :*

Incorrect : He told before we left that the invitations would be sent.

Correct   : Before we left he told that the invitations would be sent.

or

He told that the invitations would be sent before we left.

Comments : In the incorrect sentence the phrase 'before we left' may refer to 'told' or to "sent". So the sentence is ambiguous. If it is to be connected with 'told', bring it in the beginning and if with 'sent', put it at the end.

Incorrect : He announced the following day to close down the factory.

Correct   : The following day he announced to close down the factory.

or

He announced to close down the factory the following day.

In this case also 'the following day' can be connected with 'announced' or 'close down'. So the sentence is ambiguous.

Incorrect : He told after some time that he would meet the delegates.

Correct : After sometime he told that he would meet the delegates.

or

He told that he would meet the delegates after some time.

Incorrect : He promised after consulting his friends to help me.

Correct : After consulting his friends he promised to help me.

or

He promised to help me after consulting his friends

(e) An adjective is put before a noun in a normal sentence. But in some cases the adjective is put after the noun to which it refers. This is called predicative adjective. *For example :*

Incorrect : Please meet the concerned officer.

Correct : Please meet the officer concerned.

In the incorrect sentence 'concerned' means 'worried' whereas the second means the clerk who is concerned with the work.

Incorrect : These flowers smell sweetly.

Correct : These flowers smell sweet.

Predicative adjective 'sweet' is needed and not an adverb 'sweetly'. *Example :*

Incorrect : Some college teachers work hard, others take life easily.

Correct : Some college teachers work hard, others take life easy.

(f) 'Who' and 'Which' should be put immediately after the noun or pronoun which it qualifies. *Example :*

DISCIPLINE OF WRITING

Incorrect : He dropped a coin in water which he could not find.

Correct : He dropped a coin in water and he could not find it.

'Which' in the first sentence refers to 'water' so the sentence means that he could not find water. That is why it is wrong.

Incorrect : By bus we went to the college which met with an accident.

Correct : We went to the college by bus which met with an accident.

The incorrect sentence means that the 'college' met with an accident where as the 'bus' met with an accident.

Incorrect : Fine tea is in the cup which is bought from the tea garden.

Correct : Fine tea which is bought from the tea garden is in the cup.

The incorrect sentence means that the cup was bought from the tea garden.

Incorrect : The steel pins which are made of card board are in the boxes.

Correct : The steel pins are in the boxes which are made of card board.

'Pins' cannot be made of card board so 'which' refers to boxes.

(g) We cannot put an adverb by splitting an infinitive. *For example :*

Incorrect : You have been asked to quickly go there.

Correct : You have been asked to go there quickly.

The adverb *quickly* cannot be put between 'to' and 'go'.

Incorrect : He is trying to falsely implicate him in the case.

Correct : He is trying to implicate him in the case falsely.

Incorrect : I have been advised to immediately abandon the project.

Correct : I have been advised to abandon the project immediately.

Incorrect : It is difficult to completely give up this habit.

Correct : It is difficult to give up this habit completely.

Incorrect : He was ordered to suddenly go.

Correct : He was ordered to go suddenly.

Structure of Conditional Sentences

There are three types of conditional sentences :

Type 1 : In this type of a conditional sentence 'If' and 'Had' or only 'Had' is used in the "if clause" and "would have" is used in the consequent clause. *For example* :

If he had come I would have met him.
or
"Had he come I would have met him.

Type 2 : In this type of a conditional sentence 'If' and verb in present indefinite tense are used in the "if clause" and future indefinite tense is used in the consequent clause. *For example:*

If it rains I will not go out.

If it suits him he will join this firm.

Type 3 : In this type of a conditional sentence 'If' and verb in the past tense are used in the 'if clause' and generally "would" is used in the consequent clause. *For example* :

If he wasted money he would suffer.

Incorrect : If he had slept he will not take rest.

Correct : If he had slept he would not have taken rest.

Incorrect : If he will call I will go there.

Correct : If he calls I will go there.

DISCIPLINE OF WRITING

Incorrect : If he went there he will meet his old friend.
Correct : If he went there he would meet his old friend.
Incorrect : Had he finished the work he will come back.
Correct : Had he finished the work he would have come back.
Incorrect : If he chooses to retire no body objects.
Correct : If he chooses to retire no body will object.
Incorrect : If he had finished his work he would leave.
Correct : If he had finished his work he would have left.

4

Correct Use of Parts of Speech

Using Nouns

There are two types of errors concerning the use of nouns
  (i) errors in the agreement of noun and verb
  (ii) errors in the use of plurals.

Determining the Subject. Sometimes we are unable to determine the real subject and use the wrong verbs. *For example :*

Incorrect : A group of boys *were* to sing.
Correct   : A group of boys *was* to sing.

Incorrect : The memoranda *is* handed over to the Minister.
Correct   : The memoranda *are* handed over to the Minister.

In the above quoted examples 'group' is used as singular whereas 'memoranda' is plural.

Collective Nouns. When collective noun is used collectively verbs should be singular, otherwise plural.

Incorrect : The Committee *are* empowered to deal with this problem.
Correct   : The Committee *is* empowered to deal with this problem.

CORRECT USE OF PARTS OF SPEECH

In this the collective noun 'Committee' is used collectively.

Use of 'or'. Whenever two nouns or pronouns are joined by or, verb is according to the second noun or pronoun. *For example :*

Mohan or I *am* to do this work. The verb *'am'* is used because with 'I' we can use only this verb.

Double Subject. Do not use double subjects with one verb. *For example:*

Incorrect : He and I we took the wrong path.

Correct : He and I took the wrong path.

Use of 'There'. 'There' is an introductory word in a sentence, where, this word is used verb should be according to the actual subject. *For example :*

There is the boys who abused you.

This should be rewritten (because the real subject is 'boys') by using plural verb;

There are the boys who abused you.

Use of 'As Well ... As'. Whenever, two nouns or pronouns are joined by 'as well...as' verb should be according to the first noun or pronoun. *For example :*

Incorrect : I as well as he is to speak.

Correct : I as well as he am to speak.

Use of Neither...nor/Either...or. Whenever, the nouns or pronouns are joined by 'neither...nor'/'either...or' verb should agree with the second noun or pronoun. *For example :*

Incorrect : Neither he nor his brothers is happy.

Correct : Neither he nor his brothers are happy.

Incorrect : Either I or my brothers am to meet the Prime Minister.

Correct : Either I or my brothers are to meet the Prime Minister.

Use of 'Not only'. In this case also verbs should agree with the second noun or pronoun. *For example :*

Incorrect : Not only Shyam but his brothers *has* also gone out of station.

Correct : Not only Shyam but his brothers *have* also gone out of station.

Use of 'As...As' and 'So...As'. Wherever, nouns are joined with 'as...as' or 'so...as', verb is determined by the second noun or pronoun. *For example :*

Incorrect : He is careless as his subordinates is.

Correct : He is as careless as his subordinates are.

Use of 'A lot of'. When 'A lot of' refers to quantity, verb is singular, and when it refers to number or countable things, verb is plural. *For example :*

Incorrect : A lot of sugar *were* wasted.

Correct : A lot of sugar *was* wasted.

Incorrect : A lot of persons *is* invited.

Correct : A lot of persons *are* invited.

Use of 'Every one', 'Any one', 'One of the'. If any one of these is the subject verb should be singular. *For example :*

Correct : Every one of them was present there.

Correct : Any one of the friends is to arrange the party.

Correct : One of the students has failed.

Use of 'A pair of'. When we use 'a pair of' singular verb should be used.

Correct : A pair of spectacles is with me.

Plural Nouns misused as Singulars. The following words are always plural and take plural verbs.

Clothes, Goods, Plants, Proceeds, Remains, Scissors, Spectacles, Thanks, Trousers, Wages, People, Cattle.

Singular Nouns misused as Plural. The following nouns are used as singular and take singular verbs.

CORRECT USE OF PARTS OF SPEECH

Alms, Athletics, Civics, Mathematics, Economics, Measles, Mumps, News, Poetics, Politics, Whereabouts, United States.

Nouns used as Singulars and Plurals. The following words can be used as singulars as well as plurals and take verbs accordingly.

Innings, Sheep, Dozen, Dear.

Directions. *Point out which underlined part of each of the following sentences is incorrect in standard English.*

1. There have been heavy rainfall yesterday. No Error
       A   B   C   D   E

2. Herbert as well as his class fellows are playing hockey.
        A   B   C   D
   No Error
   E

3. Neither the head constable nor other policemen is
           A   B   C   D
   injured. No Error
                E

4. Every leaf and every flower proclaim the glory of God.
     A   B   C   D
   No Error
   E

5. Six miles are a long distance. No Error.
      A   B C   D   E

6. Playing the harmonium and singing are difficult.
       A   B   C   D
   No Error
   E

7. The team are out to win the match. No Error
         A   B   C   D   E

8. The cluster of grapes were plucked by the child.
      A   B   C   D
   No Error
   E

9. A box of apples are in the car. No Error
       A   B C   D   E

10. The Jury is arguing among themselves. No Error
        A   B   C   D   E

11. A good house and a good bank account are what he
    A   B   C   D
    wants. No Error
            E

12. Either he or his servant has seen a snake in the garden.
      A   B   C   D
    No Error
      E

ANSWERS

1. B	2. C	3. D	4. B
5. B	6. D	7. B	8. C
9. B	10. B	11. C	12. E

Using Tenses

1. We always use present indefinite tense when we are referring to a universal truth. *For example* :

    He said that the earth *revolves* round the sun.

2. Any action which is regularly or habitually done, is written in present indefinite tense. *For example* :

    He always *tells* lies.

    He generally *meets* him.

    I often *meet* him.

3. Double 'will' are not used in the same sentence; once present tense will be used, *For example* :

    I *will* meet you when you come back.

4. If the action is in the present we make use of present continuous tense. *For example:*

    I am *going* just now.

    He is *coming* to meet you.

5. When action continues for some time perfect continuous tense is used. *For example* :

    He *has been working* since morning.

CORRECT USE OF PARTS OF SPEECH

He *has been playing* for two hours.

I *have been thinking* about it for many months.

6. Past perfect tense is used when there are two actions, both in past tense and one earlier than the other. *For example :*

    The patient *had died* when the doctor came.

    They *had left* their house before he came.

7. Every sentence in which the word 'wish' is used or its sense is given must take one of these four verbs (i) 'had' when the man repents over the past (ii) 'were' when we wish for something impossible at present. (iii) 'would' when we refer to the future (iv) 'could' when we refer to a possibility. *For example :*

    (a) I wish I *were* a bird. (wishing impossible).

    (b) I have failed, I wish *I had* worked harder.

    (c) I wish *I would* get what I want.

    (d) They are *free* today. I wish they *could* accompany you.

8. If many things are done at the same time, same verb is used. *For example :*

    (a) I came, I saw, I conquered.

    (b) I met him, talked to him and followed him.

9. Past tense must be followed by past tense unless it is a universal truth.

10. Perfect continuous tense should be used when work continues for a long time.

Directions. *Point out which underlined part of the following sentences is not acceptable in standard English.*

1. I <u>started</u> the <u>car and</u> <u>drive</u> down <u>the</u> street. <u>NO ERROR</u>
       A   B   C   D   E

2. <u>Mary</u> <u>cut</u> Anne's <u>hair</u> and <u>curls</u> them. <u>NO ERROR</u>
      A   B   C   D   E

3. You wash the dishes and I dry them. No Error
   A   B   C   D   E

4. Now they watched the river everyday. No Error
   A   B   C   D   E

5. They often went fishing together. No Error
   A   B   C   D   E

6. He went before I left this place. No Error
   A   B   C D   E

7. If I am a king. No Error
   A B C D   E

8. I saw him when he talked to his friend. No Error
   A B   C   D   E

9. He is working for the past four hours. No Error.
   A B   C   D   E

10. I will come just now. No Error
    A B   C   D   E

11. I watched him fell. No Error
    A B   C   D   E

12. I will contact you when you will come. No Error
    A B   C   D   E

13. I told that he will come today. No Error
    A B   C   D   E

14. He will leave you in the lurch. No Error
    A B   C D   E

15. The crowd shouting and cheered. No Error
    A   B   C   D   E

ANSWERS

1. C	2. B	3. D	4. B
5. E	6. C	7. D	8. D
9. B	10. B	11. D	12. D
13. C	14. E	15. C	

Use of Prepositions

Preposition is a small word used with a noun to tell what, where, when or how. *For example :*

The men walked *on the moon.*

The phrase 'on the moon' tells where the men walked. The most common prepositions are :

AT	DOWN	ON	ACROSS
BY	FROM	TO	AFTER
IN	INTO	UP	AGAINST
OF	LIKE	FOR	ALONG
OFF	OVER	ABOVE	BEHIND
AMONG	AROUND	BEFORE	BELOW
UPON	WITH	ABOUT	EXCEPT
BESIDE	BETWEEN	DURING	UNDERNEATH
THROUGH	TOWARD	WITHOUT	

The rules regarding the use of prepositions do not help much because there is a large number of exceptions to them. Following is the list of important words followed by prepositions.

Ability *for* or in work
Access *to* a person
Accomplice *with* a person
Accomplice *in* crime
Admission *to* a person
Admission *into* place
Affection *for* a person
Affinity *with* something
Affinity *between* two things
Allusion *to* something
Ambition *for* distinction
Anxiety *for* some one's safety

Affection

Apology *for* a fault
Application *for* employment
Application *of* technology to
Approach *to* anything
Aptitude *for* science
Authority *over* a person
Authority *on* a subject
Authority *to* study
Attention *for* saying
Attack *on* a place
Bargain *with* a person
Bargain *for* a thing
Betrayal *of* a secret
Blindness *to* one' faults
Candidate *for* a seat
Care *for* his safety
Care *of* his books
Cause *for* anxiety
Cause *of* trouble
Change (noun) *of* number
Charge (verb) *with* murder
Claim *on* or against someone
Claim *to* something
Comparison *with* a person or a thing
Competition *with* a person
Competition *for* a thing
Complaint *against* a person
Complaint *about* a thing
Confidence *in* a person
Conform *with* views
Conform *to* rules

CORRECT USE OF PARTS OF SPEECH

Consideration for

Consideration *for* a person
Consideration *of* a thing
Control *over* a person or a thing
Controversy *with* a person
Controversy *on* or *about* something
Decision *on* some case
Decision *of* some dispute
Delight *in* a person
Desire *for* wealth
Disagreement *with* a person
Dissent *from* a proposal
Distrust *of* a person
Doubt *of* or about a thing
Duty *to* a person
Engagement *in* business
Engagement *with* a person
Enmity *with* a person
Escape *from* punishment

Excuse *for* a fault
Experience *of* a thing
Experience *in* doing something
Failure *of* a rain
Failure *of* a person in something
Faith *in* a person
Familiarity *with* a person
Freedom *from* care
Freedom *of* action
Gratitude *for* a thing
Gratitude *to* a person
Grief *at* an event
Grief *for* a person
Hatred *of* or *for* a person
Hatred *of* a thing
Hope (v) *for* something
Hope (n) *in* achieving
Hope (n) *of* getting,
Indifference *to* heat
Indulgence *in* wine
Indulgence *to* a person
Inference *from* facts
Inquiry *into* circumstances
Insight *into* character
Interview *with* a person
Invitation *to* dinner
Jurisdiction *over* a province
Jurisdiction *in* a law suit
Justification *of* or *for* crime

Faith in

CORRECT USE OF PARTS OF SPEECH

Lecture on

Lecture *on* a subject
Libel *on* a person
Libel *against* his character
Liking *for* a person
Longing *for* or *after* a thing
Necessity *for* anything
Necessity *of* the case
Need *for* assistance
In need *of* assistance
Neglect *of* duty
Neglect *in* doing a thing
Objection *to* a proposal
Offence *against* morality
Offence *at* something done
Order *for* or *against* doing a thing
Popularity *among* colleagues
Popularity *with* subordinates
Pity *for* sufferers
Pride *in* wealth
Readiness *at* figures

Readiness *in* answering
Readiness *for* journey
Reason *for* a thing
Reason *against* a thing
Relation *of* one thing to another
Relation *between* two things
Relation *with* a person
Request *for* something
Responsible *to* the law
Responsibility *for* action
Revolt *against* authority
Search *for* or *after* wealth
Share *of* a thing
Share *with* a person
Sympathy *with* or *for* the poor

Adjectives Followed by Prepositions

Absorbed *in* study
Accountable *to* a person
Accountable *for* a thing
Accused *of* crime
Adapted *to* his taste
Adapted *for* occupation
Afraid *of* death
Alien *to* his character
Allied *to* a thing
Allied *with* a person
Angry *at* a thing
Angry *with* a person
Annoyed *with* a person

Angry at a thing

CORRECT USE OF PARTS OF SPEECH

Annoyed *for* saying something
Anxious *for* safety
Anxious *about* the result
Ashamed *of* his dullness
Astonished *at* behaviour
Aware *of* his ambitions
Based *on* facts
Bent *on* doing
Blessed *with* good physique
Blessed *in* his children
Blind *to* his faults
Blind *of* one eye
Born *of* rich parents
Born *in* India
Careful *of* money
Charged *to* his account
Charged *with* a bullet
Charged *with* a crime
Comparable *to* that
Concerned *at* or *about* some happening
Concerned *for* a person's welfare
Concerned *in* some business
Confident *of* success
Conscious *of* fault
Contrasted *with* something
Convicted *of* crime
Contrary *to* rule
Coupled *with*
Deaf *to* requests
Deficient *in* energy
Delighted *with* success

Blessed with good physique

Deprived *of* something
Different *from* something
Disappointed *of* a thing not obtained
Disappointed *in* a thing got
Disappointed *with* a person
Distinct *from* something
Eligible *for* something
Engaged *to* a person
Engaged *in* a business
Envious *of* other's success
Familiar *with* a language
Familiar *to* a person
Fond *of* music
Free *from* blame
Good *for* nothing
Good *at* a game
Grateful *to* a person
Hungry *after* wealth
Inclined *to* something
Indebted *to* a person
Indebted *for* kindness
Indebted *in* a big thing
Informed *of* facts
Inimical *to* a person
Insensible *to* shame
Intimate *with* a person
Lame *of* one leg
Loyal *to* a person
Moved *to* tears
Moved *with* pity
Moved *at* the sight
Moved *by* requests

Negligent *of* duties
Negligent *in* work
Obliged *to* a person
Obliged *for* kindness
Occupied *with* work
Occupied *in* reading

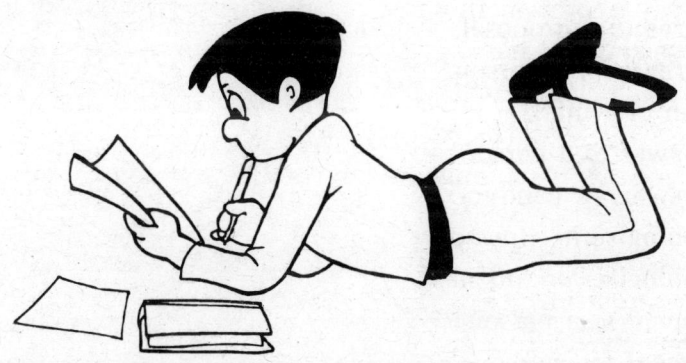

Occupied in Reading

Opposed *to* facts
Polite *to* strangers
Polite *in* habits
Popular *with* subordinates
Popular *among* equals
Quick *of* understanding
Quick *at* mathematics
Responsible *to* a person
Responsible *for* action
Slow *of* hearing
Slow *in* making plans
Slow *at* accounts
Suitable *to* the occasion
Suitable *for* his income
Tired *of* doing
Tired *with* exercise

Verbs followed by Prepositions

Abide *by* one's words
Accord *with* a person
Acquit *of* a charge
Admit *of* an excuse
Admit *to* a secret
Agree *to* a proposal
Agree *with* a person
Aim *at* a mark
Answer *to* a person
Answer *for* conduct
Apologise *to* a person
Apologise *for* rudeness
Appeal *to* a person
Appeal *for* help
Appeal *against* sentence
Apply *to* a person
Apply *for* a thing
Arrive *at* a place
Arrive *in* a country
Ask *for* a thing
Ask *from* a person
Attend *to* a lecture
Attend *on* a person
Beg *pardon* of a person
Beg *a* person to do
Beg *for* something from someone
Believe *in* one's honesty
Break *into* the house
Break *oneself* of a habit
Break *through* restraint
Break *with* a person

Break *news* to a person
Burst *into* anger
Burst *upon* a person
Call *to* a person (Shout for)
Call *on* a person
Charge *a* person with crime
Call *for* punishment
Come *into* fashion
Come *across* a person
Come *of* something
Come *by* a thing
Come *to* a particular amount
Communicate *a* thing to a person
Communicate *with* a person

Communicate with a person

Compare *to* (dissimilarities)
Compare *with* (similarities)
Consist *of* a material
Consist *in* results
Contend *with* a person
Contend *from* a thing
Deal *in* a business
Deal *with* a person

Deal with a subject
Deal *out* cards
Die *of* disease
Die *from* some work
Die *by* violence
Differ *with* a person in views
Differ *from* in appearance
Distinguish *one* thing from another
Distinguish *between* two things
Enter *upon* a career
Enter *into* one's plans
Exempt *from* tax
Explain *to* a person
Fail *in* an attempt
Fail *of* a purpose
Fall *among* thieves
Fall *in* love with a person
Fall *in* with views
Fall *on* the onomy
Fall *into* a mistake
Fall *under* displeasure
Feed *on* grass
Feed *with* grass
Fight *for* the weak
Fight *against* the strong
Fly *at* a dog
Fly *into* rage
Get *out* facts (find out)
Get *over* illness
Get *on* a person
Get *out* of debt
Get *to* a journey's end

Fall in love with a person

Glance *at* an object
Glance *over* a letter
Grieve *at* an event
Grieve *for* a person
Inform on someone to the police
Inform the accident to the police
Inquire *about* (ask)
Inquire *into* (investigate)
Invite *to* dinner
Join *in* a game
Keep *from* wine (abstain)
Keep *to* the point
Knock *someone* down
Knock *somebody's* head
Knock *at* the door
Labour *for* public good
Labour *in* a good cause
Labour *at* some work
Laugh *at* (make fun)
Laugh *with* (share fun)
Lean *against* a wall
Lean *on* a walking stick
Lean *to* an opinion
Listen *to* a complaint
Listen *for* musical notes
Live *for* fame
Live *by* honest labour
Live *on* small income
Live *within* one's means
Look *after* business
Look *at* a person
Look *into* the matter

Look *for* something
Look *over* an account
Look *through* (examine carefully)
Make *away* with money
Make *for* happiness
Make *upto* a person
Object *to* a proposal
Part *with* a person
Play *at* a game
Play *upon* musical instrument

Play upon musical instrument

Play *tricks* with
Prepare *for* the worst
Prepare *against* disaster
Prevail *over* an adversary
Prevail *with* a person (have influence)
Proceed *with* business (already started)
Proceed *to* business (not started)
Proceed *from* one point to another

Proceed *against* a person
Provide *for* children
Provide *against* bad days
Provide *oneself* with some thing
Recover *from* illness
Run *after* fashions
Run *at* (attack)

Run at

Run *into* debt
Run *over* (read rapidly)
Run *through* his money
Search *for* lost thing
Search *into* a matter
Send *for* a doctor
Set *a* person over (incharge)
Set *upon* (attack)
Sit *over* a file (delay)
Smile *at* the threats of person
Smile *on* (favour) a person
Speak *of* a subject (brief)

Speak *on* a subject
Stand *against* an enemy
Stand *by* a friend
Stand *on* dignity
Stand *to* reason
Strike *at* a dog
Strike *for* higher pay
Strike *on* a rock
Supply a thing *to* a person
Supply a person *with* a thing
Sympathise *with*
Take *after* (resemble)
Take *for* (considered to be)
Take *to* gambling
Talk *of* or *about* an event
Talk *over* a matter
Talk *to* or *with*

Talk to or with

Think *of* or *about* anything
Think *over* a matter
Trifle *with* a man's feelings
Turn *to* a friend for help
Turn *upon* evidence

CORRECT USE OF PARTS OF SPEECH

Exercise for Assimilation

Directions. *Four parts of a sentence are underlined. One of them is not acceptable in standard English Pick it out. If all underlined parts are correct mark 'E'.*

1. People <u>will</u> <u>blame</u> you <u>with</u> wasting <u>your</u> time. <u>No Error</u>
            A   B   C   D
     E

2. <u>You</u> must <u>apologise</u> <u>with</u> him <u>for</u> this. <u>No Error</u>
    A   B   C   D   E

3. I <u>have</u> bestowed a <u>great</u> attention <u>to</u> this <u>subject</u>. <u>No Error</u>
     A   B   C   D
    E

4. I am <u>with</u> the need <u>of</u> a <u>good</u> advice. <u>No Error</u>
      A B   C   D   E

5. <u>The horses</u> <u>feed</u> <u>with</u> <u>grass</u>. <u>No Error</u>
       A   B   C   D   E

6. He <u>begged</u> <u>for</u> help <u>when</u> I <u>met</u> him. <u>No Error</u>
        A   B   C   D   E

7. The <u>point</u> you <u>spoke</u> will <u>be</u> attended <u>to</u>. <u>No Error</u>
       A   B   C   D   E

8. I have <u>no</u> <u>influence</u> <u>with</u> <u>that</u> man. <u>No Error</u>
        A   B   C   D   E

9. He is <u>quite</u> weak <u>in</u> English; he should <u>work</u> hard.
       A   B   C   D
   <u>No Error</u>
    E

10. The charge <u>with</u> theft <u>is</u> levelled <u>against</u> him.
     A   B   C   D
    <u>No Error</u>
     E

11. Reputation <u>stands</u> <u>in</u> nothing <u>other</u> <u>than</u> honesty.
              A   B   C   D
    <u>No Error</u>
     E

12. You <u>must</u> have courage <u>to</u> stand <u>upon</u> requests.
        A   B   C
<u>No Error</u>
  E

13. <u>He</u> turned <u>a deaf</u> ear <u>on</u> your request. <u>No Error</u>
    A   B   C D   E

14. <u>No</u> complaint <u>has</u> <u>been</u> lodged <u>on</u> him. <u>No Error</u>
    A   B   C   D   E

15. You <u>are</u> <u>requested</u> to <u>conform</u> <u>with</u> rules. <u>No Error</u>
        A   B   C   D   E

ANSWERS

1. C	2. C	3. C	4. B
5. C	6. E	7. D	8. C
9. B	10. B	11. B	12. C
13. D	14. D	15. D	

The use of Article 'The'

Rule 1 : If the substantives are used in general sense, their names should not be preceded by 'the' article. *For example :*

Lead is considered to be the heaviest metal *(not the lead).*

Gold has a shining of its own *(not the gold).*

The gold which is smuggled is not of good quality *(not gold).*

The lead which you found here has been brought from Bombay *(not lead only)*

Rule 2 : Article 'the' is not used even before the meals if they refer to the meals in general. *For example :*

We take breakfast at 9.00 a.m. (not the breakfast)

I do not think you have taken your lunch. *(not the lunch)*

The breakfast which was given by him was quite good. *(the* is used because it refers to a particular breakfast)

Rule 3 : If the word king or queen is followed by the name, 'the' is not used. *For example :*

It is incorrect to say the king George II or the Edward VII, but otherwise 'the' is used with king or queen while referring to a particular king or queen.

Rule 4 : 'The' is not put before the name of the games. *For example :*

It is incorrect to say that "I like to play the football".

Rule 5 : 'The' is put before the nouns which refer to the inhabitants of a country but not before the names of their languages. *For example :*

The English are considered to be religious people. (it refers to people)

English is a very rich language. (reference is to language).

Rule 6: "The' is put before the names of the mountains, hills, and also rivers, canals, valleys, forests, etc. *For example :*

1. The Himalayas lie in the north of India.
2. London is on the bank of the Thames.
3. We crossed the Pacific Ocean in that ship.

The Indefinitive Articles 'a' and 'an'

Rule 1 : The article 'a' is used before words beginning with a consonant and 'an' before words beginning with vowels or with letter 'h' if 'h' is silent. *For example :*

'An'. will be used with the honest, honorary, etc.

Rule 2 : Article 'a' or 'an' must be used before singular nouns which stand for such things as can be counted. *For example :*

A cow is an animal.
Wheat is considered to be a cereal.

Rule 3 : An indefinite article must be used when the noun is preceded by an adjective. *For example :*

India is a big country.
He is a good-hearted fellow.

Rule 4 : An indefinite article should always be used with the names of professions and occupations. *For example :*

Her husband is a teacher in this college.

He has joined medical college with the hope to become a doctor.

Rule 5 : 'An' article must be placed after the word *"such"* when the latter refers to the things that can be counted. *For example :*

I have never seen such a strange person. (*not such strange person*).

Rule 6 : When the article 'a' is used with the word *"few"* it means 'some' whereas, only 'few' means 'no one'. *For example :*

Few people are able to cast vote properly. (it means no person)

A few answers given by the students were correct. (that means some)

Rule 7 : When article 'a' is used with 'little' it means 'some' and when no article is used, it means nothing. *For example :*

Little progress has been made by the Planning Commission.

A little hint will help us in understanding the problem properly (it means some)

Omission of Articles

Rule 1 : The article is omitted before a proper noun. That means no article will be used with Mumbai, Delhi, etc. But when an article is used before proper noun, it becomes a common noun. *For example :*

Kalidas is the Shakespeare of India.

Kashmir is the Switzerland of India.

Rule 2 : An article is omitted before a plural noun, which stands for a class of people. *For example :*

Historians generally commit mistakes. Politicians have their own ends to serve.

CORRECT USE OF PARTS OF SPEECH

Rule 3 : An article is omitted before a material and abstract noun when they are used in a general sense. *For example :*

Iron is a useful metal. (not *the iron*)
Virtue has its own reward. (not *the virtue*)

Rule 4 : Articles are omitted before the names of diseases and the regular meals. *For example :*

He is suffering from malaria (not *the malaria*).
He took his dinner a short while ago. (not *the dinner*)
Hell is paved with gold. (not *the hell*)

Rule 5 : Articles are omitted before a noun which comes after 'kind of' or 'sort of'. *For example :*

What kind of paper is this? (Not 'kind of a paper')
What sort of businessman is he? (not a *businessman*)

Rule 6 : Article is omitted before adjectives used as nouns and refers to languages and colours. *For example :*

He liked blue and yellow colours. (not the blue or the yellow)

Use of Adjective

Rule 1 : The verbs *"to be, to seem, to become"* are followed by an adjective and not by an adverb. *For example :*

Incorrect : After the rain the weather turned *warmly*.
Correct   : After the rain the weather turned warm.

Rule 2 : Some of the verbs *"like turn, grow, appear"* do not mean *become* or *seem* so with them adverb may be used. *For example :*

Incorrect : While running he turned round quick.
Correct   : While running he turned round quickly.

Rule 3 : Generally words ending with 'ly' are adverbs but words like *brotherly, fatherly, homely, lovely, womanly* can be used as adjectives. *For example :*

He talks in a *gentlemanly* manner.

This is a *lovely* scene.

His *manly* approach is appreciated.

Rule 4 : *Hard, Late* and *Most* are adjectives and must be used as adjectives. *For example :*

He is *hard* pressed for time.

Old habits die *hard*.

Rule 5 : Adjectives in the comparative degree and ending with 'ior' (inferior, superior, senior, junior) take *'To'* and not *'Than'*. *For example :*

My pen is *superior* to his.

He is *inferior* to me.

Rule 6 : Double comparatives and superlatives cannot be used in modern English. *For example :*

This book is *more preferable* to that. (incorrect)

This book is *preferable* to that.

Rule 7 : When comparative degree is used in the superlative sense it must be followed by 'any other' and not by 'any'. *For example :*

This newspaper is *better than any other* in the country.

He is *tougher than any other* person in the country.

Rule 8 : ELDER; OLDER — *Elder* is used for persons belonging to the same family or class, *Older* is used while comparing the age of different persons. *For example :*

My brother is *elder* to me by two years.

Rule 9 : While comparing two things, we should compare the two things only. *For example :*

1. This house is better than Ram.   (Incorrect)
   This house is better than *that of Ram*.   (Correct)

2. The speed of the new car is higher than the old one.   (Incorrect)
   The speed of the new car is higher than *that of the old one*.   (Correct)

CORRECT USE OF PARTS OF SPEECH

Rule 10 : If one of the adjectives is used in the superlative the other should also be superlative. *For example* :

1. He is the most intelligent and hard working man. (Incorrect)

   He is the most intelligent and *the most hardworking* man. (Correct)

2. He is the most popular and shrewd politician. (Incorrect)

   He is the most popular and the most shrewd politician. (Correct)

Rule 11 : We cannot use words like —

"eternal, parallel, circular, complete, perfect, entire empty, full, preferable, round, impossible, infinite."

in the comparative or superlative degree.

Rule 12 : An adjective in the superlative degree is preceded by the article 'the'. *For example* :

He is the *best* student of the class. (Correct)

This is a *most* unworthy act. (Incorrect)

Rule 13 : For comparing two things or persons make use of comparative degree only. *For example* :

1. He is the tallest of the two. (Incorrect)
   He is taller of the two. (Correct)

2. Out of these two books this is the most enjoyable. (Incorrect)

   Out of these two books this is more enjoyable. (Correct)

Rule 14 : LESS and FEW — *"Less"* is used for quantity and *"few"* for countable number. *For example* :

1. There are *less* books in the library. (Incorrect)
   There are a *few* books in the library. (Correct)

2. There were *less* students in the class. (Incorrect)

There were a *less* number of students in the class.
(Correct)

or

These were a *few* students in the class.   (Correct)

Rule 15 : LAST and LATEST, LATER and LATTER — The words *'later'* and *'latest'* refer to time while *'last'* and *'latter'* refer to position. *'Latest'* means the most recent, whereas, *'later'* is the comparative degree of late. *'Latter'* means the one mentioned after something and *'last'* means something after which nothing comes. *For example :*

1. The later information is correct but the earlier was not.   (Correct)
2. This was his *last* wish.   (Correct)
3. The *latter* chapters of this book are useful. (Correct)

Rule 16 : FEW and A FEW; LITTLE and A LITTLE — *Little* and *few* are negative adjectives which mean not many. A *little* and a *few* mean some at least. *For example :*

1. *Little* money was left with him.(Correct; meaning *not much*)
2. A *little* effort is needed.   (Correct; means *some*)
3. *Few* problems were easy. (Correct; means *not many*)
4. A few persons had come to visit the fair.
(Correct; means *some*)

Rule 17 : BOTH — We cannot write "the both books, the both parents" etc. *Both* should not be used in a negative sentence. *For example :*

1. The both brothers were convicted.   (Incorrect)
   Both the brothers were convicted.   (Correct)
2. Both of them did not arrive in time.   (Incorrect)
   Neither of them arrived in time.   (Correct)

Rule 18 : Use of ONE OF — If an adjective follows the phrase *one of*, it should be in superlative. *For example :*

CORRECT USE OF PARTS OF SPEECH

1. He is *one of* the great personalities. (Incorrect)
   He is one of *the greatest* personalities. (Correct)
2. Delhi is one of the more populated cities.
   (Not good English)
   Delhi is one of the most populated cities.

Rule 19 : Use of 'MANY A' — The phrase *many a* means the plural subject but is followed by a singular verb. *For example :*

Many students have been arrested. (Correct)
Many a student has been arrested. (Correct)

Exercise

Instructions. *Which underlined part in each of the following sentences is NOT acceptable in standard English. If all are acceptable then mark "no error."*

1. Of the books which is least costly. No Error
   A   B   C   D   E

2. This is the most ideal suggestion that you have given.
   A   B   C   D
   No Error
   E

3. My house is decidedly better than John. No Error
   A   B   C   D   E

4. There were no less than forty persons in the hall.
   A   B   C   D
   No Error
   E

5. To some death is more preferable to begging. No Error
   A   B   C   D   E

6. The man who is promoted is junior than me. No Error
   A   B   C   D   E

7. The latest chapters of this book are not so interesting.
   A   B   C   D
   No Error
   E

8. Perhaps you know that Delhi is a worth seeing place.
       A   B   C   D
   No Error / E

9. Our teacher has told us that this is a best book on the subject. No Error
                A   B   C   D   E

10. He has gone to his older brother who is a doctor. No Error
         A   B   C   D   E

11. There is no any man who can help me. No Error
      A   B   C   D   E

12. The two first chapters of this book are well written. No Error
      A   B   C   D   E

13. I do not accept it because it is the most extreme view. No Error
      A   B   C   D   E

14. This rule is of the most universal application. No Error
      A   B   C   D   E

15. Kalidas is greater than any writer of Sanskrit dramas. No Error
                 A   B   C   D   E

Answers

1. A	2. B	3. D	4. B	5. B
6. D	7. B	8. D	9. C	10. C
11. B	12. B	13. C	14. C	15. B

CORRECT USE OF PARTS OF SPEECH

Use of Adverb

An *adverb* tells us something more about the verb. When we say "He runs fast" the word *fast* is adverb.

Rule 1 : Adverbs denoting time :

always, never, often, sometimes, generally, seldom, merely are placed before the verb which they qualify. *Example :*

1. We *often* go to meet him. (Correct)
2. I *seldom* talk to him. (Correct)
3. I *never* said this. (Correct)

Rule 2 : Double negatives should not be used if we want to say something negative. *Example :*

1. I forbade him *not* to go. (Incorrect)
   I forbade him *to* go. (Correct)
2. Work *lest* you *should not* fail. (Incorrect)
   Work lest you *should* fail. (Correct)
3. I could *not hardly* walk. (Incorrect)
   I could *hardly* walk. (Correct)

Rule 3 : MUCH; VERY — (a) *Much* is used to qualify adjectives or adverbs in the comparative degree and *very* when these are in the positive degree.

(b) *Much* is used with past participles and *very* with present participle. *Very* is used with past participle when the latter is used as an adjective. *Example :*

1. He is *much* better now. (Correct)
2. He is *very* happy these days. (Correct)
3. This is *much* advanced study. (Correct)
4. This is a *very* interesting book. (Correct)

Rule 4 : TOO — The adverb 'too' which means *more than enough* should not be used for *very* or *much*. *Example :*

1. It is *too* difficult. (Incorrect)
   It is *very* difficult. (Correct)
2. I am *too* happy to meet you. (Incorrect)
   I am *very* happy to meet you. (Correct)

Rule 5 : ELSE — The adverb *else* should be followed by *but* and not by *than*. *Example :*

It is nothing *else* but humility. (Correct)

Rule 6 : HARD, HARDLY — *Hard* is an adverb and *Hardly* means *scarcely*. *Example :*

Old habits die *hard*. (Correct)

Hardly could I believe this. (Correct)

Rule 7: NO, NOT — *No* is an adjective whereas *Not* is an adverb. *Example :*

I am *not* hoping against hope. (Correct)

No work was done by him. (Correct)

Exercise for Assimilations

Directions. *Pick from the underlined parts which is not acceptable in standard English. If all are correct mark 'E'.*

1. <u>This</u> painting <u>is</u> <u>very much</u> <u>beautiful</u>. <u>No Error</u>
     A   B   C   D   E

2. He <u>does</u> not <u>take</u> anything he <u>only</u> <u>drinks</u> water.
        A   B   C   D
   <u>No Error</u>
     E

3. I <u>never</u> borrowed <u>your</u> book yesterday; <u>you</u> must <u>have</u> misplaced it. <u>No Error</u>
       A   B   C   D
                   E

4. He is <u>nothing</u> else <u>than</u> <u>a</u> dishonest <u>fellow</u>. <u>No Error</u>
           A   B C   D   E

5. <u>I</u> seldom or <u>ever</u> go <u>to</u> meet him. <u>No Error</u>
    A   B   C   E

6. Please <u>kindly</u> help <u>us</u> <u>at</u> this time <u>of</u> difficulty.
           A   B C   D
   <u>No Error</u>
     E

7. <u>Only</u> write <u>on</u> one side <u>of</u> <u>the</u> paper. <u>No Error</u>
     A   B   C D   E

CORRECT USE OF PARTS OF SPEECH

8. He is somewhat tall for his age. No Error
   A   B   C   D   E

9. He always arrives lately and must be punished.
         A   B   C   D
   No Error
   E

10. He walks very fastly so he may win the prize.
       A   B   C   D
    No Error
    E

Answers

| 1. C | 2. C | 3. A | 4. B | 5. B |
| 6. A | 7. A | 8. E | 9. B | 10. B |

Use of Participle

Rule 1 : Participle is a double Part of speech i.e, a verb as well as an adjective. *For example :*

As a part of finite verb we may say "I shall be loving" and as an adjective we may say "Let bygones be bygones."

Rule 2 : If the verb is transitive, the past participle is never used in active voice. *For example :*

This much-liked reader proved to be useless.

If the verb is intransitive, the past participle is not used at all. But whenever it is used it comes before the noun and not after it. *For example :*

A failed candidate, a departed lover, etc.

Rule 3 : The past participle of verbs is some times used to express permanent habit or character. *For example :*

A well-read man or a hot-headed person.

Rule 4 : The implied meaning of the participle may be 1. time 2. cause or reason, 3. condition, 4. concession. *For example :*

1. Walking along the road, I met an old friend (it should be *while* I was walking),
2. Being tired with hard work, he took rest. (cause or reason).

Use of Tag Questions

Tag question is always attached with a statement in order to confirm or deny it. For example when we say — He has gone to Mumbai. Hasn't he ? In this sentence 'hasn't he' is a tag question, which wants to confirm whether he has gone or he has not gone.

With regard to the use of a tag question, three things should be kept in mind.

(a) Tag question must be in the negative if the statement is affirmative and in the affirmative if the statement is negative.

(b) The pronoun with the tag question should be the same which has been used in the statement.

(c) The verb in the tag question should also be the same as has been used in the statement. *For example :*

(1) He has done his work. Hasn't he ?

(The verb 'has' and the pronoun 'he' and the negative 'not' make the tag question correct).

(2) He will listen to me. Won't he ?

(The verb 'will' pronoun 'he' and negative are used according to the rules).

Correlative Words and Phrases

Rule 1 : The *same* is generally followed by either *that* or *as*; For example :

1. This is the *same* peon *that* came a few days ago.
2. This is the *same* kind of remark *as* was made by his officer.

CORRECT USE OF PARTS OF SPEECH

Rule 2 : *As* is generally followed by *so*. For example :

As you sow, *so* shall you reap.

Rule 3 : *As* is followed by *as* when the sentence is affirmative and *to* is followed by *as* when the sentence is negative. For example :

1. I am not *so* stubborn *as* you consider me to be.
2. I am *as* healthy *as* I ever was.

Rule 4 : *No sooner* is always followed by *than*. For example :

No sooner had he reached the station *than* the train arrived.

Rule 5 : *Scarcely* is followed by *before*. For example :

We had *scarcely* reached the station, *before* the train started.

Rule 6 : *Hardly* is followed by *when*. For example :

We had *hardly* gone to the bazar *when* it began to rain.

Rule 7 : Not *only* is followed by *but also*. For example :

Not *only* is he honest but also good-hearted.

Rule 8 : *Though* is generally followed by *yet*. For example :

Though he has not done his work, *yet* he will go to school.

5
Bricks That Build

Words are the pegs on which you hang your ideas. They can beautify your writing, make your language forceful and help you to present your ideas correctly. English language is perhaps the richest language as far as vocabulary is concerned. Many words have similar meanings. You have to know the difference in their meanings and usage. Your vocabulary or the knowledge of words should be quivered, otherwise you may fail to express yourself. This requires vast reading, regular collection of new words and practising their use. In the following pages we give a spur to your thinking and working in this direction.

BOX 1
obedient, yielding, dutiful, subservient, submissive

OBEDIENT means *one who obeys*
    Usage : He is so obedient that he will not go against your orders.

YIELDING means *one who easily submits.*
    Usage : He is yielding by nature and not stubborn.

DUTIFUL means *one who cares for his duty.*
    Usage : He is dutiful and does not shirk work.

SUBSERVIENT means *subordinate; not very important*
    Usage : These schemes are subservient to the major plan which we chalked out.

BRICKS THAT BUILD

SUBMISSIVE means *one who submits to others' wishes.*
   Usage : A typical Indian woman is submissive by nature.

Exercise For Assimilation

Directions. *Pair the words given in Column I with meanings given in Column II.*

Column I	Column II
1. Yielding	(a) bound by duty
2. Subservient	(b) subordinate
3. Dutiful	(c) easily submits

Answers

1. (c)   2. (b)   3. (a)

BOX 2

noisy, vociferous, clamorous, boisterous, blare, resonance, harmony

NOISY means *making much noise.*
   Usage : This group of girls is noisy and so a source of disturbance.

VOCIFEROUS means *one who is quite vocal in demanding or saying something.*
   Usage : The workers are quite vociferous, we cannot silence them so easily.

CLAMOROUS means *noisy specially in demanding something.*
   Usage : The students as well as teachers were quite clamorous in getting their grievances redressed.

BOISTEROUS means *wild and noisy.*
   Usage : The winners were quite boisterous in celebrating their victory.

BLARE means *too much and jarring noise of a loud speaker.*
   Usage : Early in the morning, the loud speakers start blaring.

RESONANCE means *echo* or *resounding*
  Usage : Resonance is not the real sound, it is an induced one.

HARMONY means *produces pleasing effect.*
  Usage : If there is no harmony, the sounds become jarring.

Exercise for Assimilation

Directions. *Pair the meanings given in Column II with the words given in Column I.*

Column I	*Column II*
1. Harmony	(a) vocal
2. Clamorous	(b) wild in noise
3. Boisterous	(c) jarring sound
4. Blare	(d) induced sound
5. Resonance	(e) noisy demand
6. Vociferous	(f) agreement in sounds

Answers

1. (f) 2. (e) 3. (b) 4. (c) 5. (d)
6. (a)

BOX 3

> behold, gaze, inspect, watch, stare, observe, discern, spy, survey

BEHOLD means *to see*
  Usage : I could behold the whole scene though I was at a distance.

GAZE means *to see by fixing one's eyes* on *something.*
  Usage : The mother was gazing at the dead child.

INSPECT means *to survey or examine closely*
  Usage : After inspecting the arrangement, the officer called all the workers.

BRICKS THAT BUILD

WATCH means *to look out*
  Usage : The spectators were watching the game when the bomb blasted.

STARE means *to look fixedly*
  Usage : The boys were staring at the girls.

OBSERVE means *to note systematically*
  Usage : I can observe even from here that a foreigner is handing over a bag to the officer.

DISCERN means *to make out* or *discriminating*
  Usage : His discerning eye could discover the truth.

SPY means *a person who secretly collects information about another person, country, firm*
  Usage : A foreigner was arrested on the charge of spying.

SURVEY means *to view*
  Usage : After surveying the whole area they prepared a plan for development.

Exercise for Assimilation

Directions. *Pair the words given in the first column with the meanings given in the second column.*

Column I	*Column II*
1. Watch	(a) looking fixedly at a thing
2. Stare	(b) to see
3. Gaze	(c) discriminating
4. Behold	(d) examine closely
5. Discern	(e) look fixedly at a person
6. Inspect	(f) note systematically
7. Observe	(g) to look out

Answers

1. (g)   2. (e)   3. (a)   4. (b)   5. (c)
6. (d)   7. (f)

BOX 4

subjugation, thraldom, bondage, forced labour, submission, drudgery, servitude, captivity

SUBJUGATION means *to make subordinate*
  Usage : They had to use great force in order to subjugate the rebels.

THRALDOM means *slavery*
  Usage : Thraldom even to one's whims is intolerable.

BONDAGE means *subjection to constraint*
  Usage : Bondage to customs is not good.

FORCED LABOUR means *bonded labour*
  Usage : No one can retain forced labour according to the laws of the land.

SUBMISSION means *yielding*
  Usage : For a nation which initiates a war, submission is insulting.

DRUDGERY means *dull, uninteresting work unwillingly done*
  Usage : The drudgery of the house-hold work upsets many housewives.

SERVITUDE means *subjection*
  Usage : Service howsoever glorified it may be, is nothing more than servitude.

CAPTIVITY means *the state of being a prisoner*
  Usage : If you keep any animal in captivity, its behaviour undergoes a change.

Exercise for Assimilation

Directions. *Pick up words for blank spaces in the following sentences from the box.*

1. ...... of the enemy will end the trading of threats.
2. ...... to customs is foolishness.

BRICKS THAT BUILD

3. Many animals are kept in ...... by some persons.
4. The ...... of the work is not liked by anyone.
5. It shows no freedom of thought. It is only........

Answers
1. Subjugation   2. Thraldom   3. Captivity
4. Drudgery   5. Servitude.

BOX 5

emancipation, liberty, independence, parole, extrication, release, manumission, unleash

EMANCIPATION means *freedom from social customs etc.*
  Usage : We must fight for the emancipation of the women.

LIBERTY means *freedom from the external control*
  Usage : The criminal was set at liberty.

INDEPENDENCE means *freedom from the external control*
  Usage : India got independence in 1947.

PAROLE means *some days of freedom allowed to the prisoners*
  Usage : One of the prisoners who was on parole has not returned.

EXTRICATION means *to free a person from entanglement*
  Usage : Labourers were extricated from the debris of the collapsed building.

RELEASE means *to set a prisoner free*
  Usage : Many prisoners were released from the jail.

MANUMISSION means *release from slavery*
  Usage : A freedom-loving person will always fight for manumission.

UNLEASH means *free from a leash*
  Usage : The angry guard unleashed his thong.

Exercise for Assimilation

Directions. *Pair the words given in Column I with the meanings given in Column II.*

Column I	Column II
1. Parole	(a) set at liberty
2. Extrication	(b) absence of curbs
3. Emancipation	(c) release from slavery
4. Release	(d) freedom from entanglement
5. Manumission	(e) freedom from social curbs
6. Liberty	(f) a few days of freedom to prisoners

Answers

1. (f) 2. (d) 3. (e) 4. (a) 5. (c) 6. (b)

BOX 6

> ignore, reject, veil, bypass, overlook, blind to

IGNORE means *to leave out of account*
   Usage : The persecutors ignored the pleas of the victim.

REJECT means *to refuse* to *accept*
   Usage : The U.N. rejected the proposal of the big powers.

VEIL means *material* to *cover face* or *head*. Metaphorically, it means *not in clear terms*
   Usage : Many veiled threats were given to the minister.

BY-PASS means *to side track*
   Usage : I cannot by-pass this decision of yours.

OVERLOOK means to *fail* to *notice* or *take into account.*
   Usage : A father should not overlook the legitimate demands of the children.

BLIND TO means *ignorant of*
   Usage : A judicious person should not be blind to his weaknesses.

BRICKS THAT BUILD

Exercise for Assimilation

Directions. *Pair the words in Column I with their meanings in Column II.*

Column I	Column II
1. Ignore	(a) refuse to accept
2. Veil	(b) fail to notice
3. Overlook	(c) ignorant of
4. Blind to	(d) leave out of account
5. Reject	(e) material to cover face

Answers

1. (d)   2. (e)   3. (b)   4. (c)   5. (a)

BOX 7

> slack, indolent, slothful, indifferent, unfaithful, disloyal, lazy

SLACK means *lazy* or *inactive*
   Usage : Do not be slack in performing your duties.

INDOLENT means *lazy*
   Usage : He is so indolent that he goes on postponing decision.

SLOTHFUL means *inactive* or *lazy*
   Usage : Slothful people often miss good opportunities in life.

INDIFFERENT means *not taking interest*
   Usage : I am quite indifferent to their personal problems.

UNFAITHFUL means *not loyal*
   Usage : You should not depend on an unfaithful friend.

DISLOYAL means *not faithful*
   Usage : I cannot be disloyal to my friends.

LAZY means *a person unwilling to work*
   Usage : Lazy people never make a headway in life.

Exercise for Assimilation

Directions. *Words are given in Column I. Pick up their antonyms from the box and write against each word.*

Column I	Column II
1. Interested	....
2. Active	....
3. Devoted	....
4. Prompt	....

Answers

1. Indifferent   2. Slothful   3. Disloyal   4. Slack

BOX 8

conceived, visionary, unreal, imaginary, fictitious, fanciful, illusory spurious, fake, forge

CONCEIVED means *formed* in mind or *imagined*
   Usage : He conceived this plan after studying the conditions in India.

VISIONARY means *not real* or *fanciful*
   Usage : He is a visionary. So idealistic.

UNREAL means *not real*
   Usage : I can say with certainty that the picture of the situation painted by him was unreal.

IMAGINARY means *based* on *imagination*
   Usage : These are imaginary fears and do not exist in reality.

FICTITIOUS means *concocted* or *cooked* up
   Usage : His excuses are fictitious and not real.

BRICKS THAT BUILD 79

FANCIFUL means *imaginative*
   Usage : His plans are too fanciful to be implemented.
ILLUSORY means *based* on *false idea*
   Usage : It is all illusory, free from realism.
SPURIOUS means *which is not genuine*
   Usage : Spurious medicines are freely sold in the market.
FAKE means *falsely prepared*
   Usage : Fake goods cannot be distinguished from the real ones.
FORGE means *to falsely prepar esp. documents.*
   Usage : The forged documents were submitted by the candidates.

Exercise for Assimilation

Directions. Pair the words given in Column I with their meanings given in Column II.

Column I	Column II
1. Spurious	(a) based on illusion
2. Forge	(b) formed in mind
3. Fictitious	(c) imaginative
4. Illusory	(d) falsely prepared
5. Fanciful	(e) fake
6. Conceived	(f) cooked up

Answers
1. (e)   2. (d)   3. (f)   4. (a)   5. (c)
6. (b)

BOX 9

different, multitudinous, numerous, variegated, sundry, manifold, multiform, several

DIFFERENT means *not similar*
   Usage : My views are quite different from yours.

MULTITUDINOUS means a *great number of*
   Usage : The multitudinous problems facing the country are difficult to solve.

NUMEROUS means *large* in *number*
   Usage : Numerous suggestions have been given by the members of the group.

VARIEGATED means *of great variety*
   Usage : The variegated colours of the different flowers attracted every one.

SUNDRY means *various* or *several*
   Usage : The sundry problems facing the country are colossal.

MANIFOLD means a *large number of, many times*
   Usage : Manifold opinions regarding economic development are irreconciliable.

MULTIFORM means *having many forms*
   Usage : Resentment can assume multiforms — agitation, non-co-operation, strike etc.

SEVERAL means *many*
   Usage : Several attempts have been made to overcome the dissenting groups.

Exercise for Assimilation

Directions. *Pair the words given in the first column with its meanings given in the second column.*

Column I	*Column II*
1. Several	(a) several in number
2. Numerous	(b) many times
3. Variegated	(c) a number of
4. Sundry	(d) of great variety
5. Manifold	(e) having many forms
6. Multiform	(f) many
7. Different	(g) large in number
8. Multitudinous	(h) having no similarity

BRICKS THAT BUILD

Answers

1. (f) 2. (g) 3. (d) 4. (a) 5. (b)
6. (e) 7. (h) 8. (c)

BOX 10

> stubborn, mutinous, intractable, refractory, fanatic, bigot

STUBBORN means a *person who* is *inflexible* or *obstinate*
  Usage : A stubborn person will not be able to adjust with others.

MUTINOUS means *rebellious* or *insubordinate*
  Usage : He will not compromise with his principles, even though he is mutinous.

INTRACTABLE means *stubborn*
  Usage : You cannot persuade him because he is intractable.

REFRACTORY means *stubborn* or *rebellious*
  Usage : The refractory attitude will not help you much.

FANATIC means one *who sticks* to a *religion* or *ideology blindly*
  Usage : Only fanatics can adopt the path of militancy.

BIGOT means *obstinate; adherent*
  Usage : It is difficult to change the opinion of a bigot.

Exercise for Assimilation

Directions. Words are given in Column I. Pick up their antonyms from the box and write in the blank space opposite each word.

WORDS	ANTONYMS
1. Flexible	....
2. Submissive	....
3. Yielding	....
4. Open minded	....
5. Unprejudiced	....
6. Tractable	....

Answers

1. Stubborn   2. Mutinous   3. Refractory
4. Bigot   5. Fanatic   6. Intractable

BOX 11

exceptional, extraordinary, singular, dissimilar, phenomenal, marvellous

EXCEPTIONAL means *unusual*
  Usage : There is nothing common place about it; it is exceptional.

EXTRAORDINARY means *more than ordinary*
  Usage : This work needs extraordinary effort.

SINGULAR means *that which can be singled out*
  Usage : It is a singular example of ignoring such urgent orders.

DISSIMILAR means *not identical*
  Usage : The two ideologies are dissimilar in many respects.

PHENOMENAL means *that which becomes a phenomenon*
  Usage : This country has made phenomenal progress during the last decade.

MARVELLOUS means *wonderful*
  Usage : This was a marvellous achievement of my friend.

Exercise for Assimilation

Directions. *Words in Column I can go with words given in Column II. Pair them correctly.*

Column I	Column II
1. Extraordinary	(a) Attempt
2. Exceptional	(b) Scene
3. Phenomenal	(c) Fear
4. Marvellous	(d) Case
5. Singular	(e) Progress

Answers

1. (c) 2. (d) 3. (e) 4. (b) 5. (a)

BOX 12

> actual, demonstrable, genuine, positive, veritable, essential, certain, authentic, sincere

ACTUAL means *real, not artificial*

   Usage : No body can distinguish the actual and imitation.

DEMONSTRABLE means *that which can be shown or demonstrated*

   Usage : Such deep emotions are not demonstrable.

GENUINE means *real and not fake*

   Usage : All genuine problems will be listened to.

POSITIVE means *explicitly stated*

   Usage : This is a positive proposal with no ambiguity.

VERITABLE means *true* or *properly so called*

   Usage : The life of a worker is a veritable hell.

ESSENTIAL means *necessary*

   Usage : At least essential work must be completed.

CERTAIN means *definite.*

   Usage : I am certain that I will win.

AUTHENTIC means genuine

   Usage : I have gathered this information from the authentic sources.

SINCERE means *earnest*

   Usage: You must make a sincere effort to pass the examination.

Exercise for Assimilation

Directions. *Words given in Column I can go with words in Column II. Pair them correctly.*

Column I	Column II
1. Authentic	(a) Assertion
2. Sincere	(b) Commodity
3. Veritable	(c) Image
4. Essential	(d) Need
5. Demonstrable	(e) Hell
6. Actual	(f) Source
7. Positive	(g) Effort

Answers

1. (f) 2. (g) 3. (e) 4. (b) 5. (d)
6. (c) 7. (a)

BOX 13

> priority, posterity, simultaneous, nascent, budding, young, blooming, frequent, regularity, recurrent

PRIORITY means *precedence of* or *primary importance*
 Usage : Priority must be given to those things which are essential for life.

POSTERITY means *following generations*
 Usage : If we ignore our duty, posterity will blame us.

SIMULTANEOUS means *side by side*
 Usage : The two decisions were taken simultaneously.

NASCENT means *newly emerging*
 Usage : The international situation demands that the nascent nations should remain non-aligned.

BUDDING means *newly blooming*
 Usage : The budding problems will have to be tackled before they become unconquerable.

BRICKS THAT BUILD

YOUNG means *not far-advanced in age*
  Usage : Nowadays the young are misguided by the politicians.

BLOOM means *grow to its prime*
  Usage : The young girls bloomed during their stay on the farm.

FREQUENT means *happening often* or *again and again*
  Usage : His frequent visits to this place have created doubts in the minds of all.

REGULARITY means *act of doing something regularly*
  Usage : He has maintained regularity in attending the office.

RECURRENT means *happening again and again*
  Usage : The recurrent demands made on me cannot be always met.

Exercise for Assimilation

Directions. *Pick up one word from those given in the brackets to complete each of the following sentences.*

1. He is famous for punctuality and (frequency, recurrence, regularity).
2. The (recurrent, regularity, frequency) riots have vitiated the atmosphere.
3. The present generation may not blame us but (posterity, priority, chronology) will.
4. The super-powers try to make the (nascent, budding, young) nations their pawns.
5. You must fix the (posterity, nascent, priority) before taking up this plan.
6. (Budding, Nascent, Simultaneous) attacks from two sides was made.

Answers

1. regularity 2. recurrent 3. posterity
4. nascent 5. priority 6. simultaneous.

BOX 14

> laborious, attentive, assiduous, dedicated, ardent, painstaking

LABORIOUS means *hard working*
  Usage : He will finish the work because he is laborious.

ATTENTIVE means one *who pays a lot of attention*
  Usage : You must be attentive in your classroom.

ASSIDUOUS means *persevering*
  Usage : Only assiduous persons can achieve their aim.

DEDICATED means *devoted*
  Usage : He is dedicated to social work.

ARDENT means *enthusiastic*
  Usage : He has an ardent desire to meet his old friend.

PAINSTAKING means with a *lot of labour*
  Usage : The captain played a painstaking innings.

Exercise for Assimilation

Directions. *Pick up words from the words given in brackets to complete each of the following sentences.*

1. He is not intelligent but (ardent, laborious).
2. He (assiduously, ardently) wished to get this post.
3. He is (attentive, dedicated) to social work.
4. He played a (dedicated, painstaking) innings.
5. Those who remain (ardent, attentive) will understand my lecture.

Answers

1. laborious 2. ardently 3. dedicated
4. painstaking 5. attentive.

BRICKS THAT BUILD

SECTION 2
Meanings of Important Words

Abase – to degrade
Abash – to embarrass
Abate – to decrease
Aberration – variation
Abeyance – temporary suspension
Abject – miserable
Abjure – to renounce
Ablution – cleansing
Abnegate – to reject
Abominate – to hate
Aborigine – original inhabitant
Abortive – futile
Abrogate – abolish
Absolve – to acquit
Absolution – forgiveness
Abstemious – sparing in diet
Abtruse – difficult to understand
Abut – to adjoin
Accolade – praise
Accoutre – to equip
Acerbity – bitterness
Acolyte – assistant
Acrimony – bitterness
Actuary – insurance
Actuate – to incite
Acumen – shrewdness
Adage – proverb
Adamant – inflexible
Adduce – to bring forth proof
Adipose – fatty
Adjunct – attachment

Abject

Adipose

Adjure – demand
Admonish – warn
Adroit – skilled
Adulation – praise
Adumbration – omen, warning
Adventitious – accidental
Affable – friendly
Affinity – relationship
Affluent – plentiful
Agglomerate – to gather into mass
Aggrandize – increase
Agnostic – doubter
Agrarian – Rural
Alacrity – speed
Alchemy – medieval chemistry
Allay – calm
Allude – to refer
Altercate – quarrel
Altruism – unselfishness
Amatory – loving

Amatory

Ambidextrous – versatile
Ambrosia – food for gods
Ambulant – able to walk

Ameliorate – to improve
Amenable – submissive
Amenity – pleasing manner
Amnesty – pardon
Amulet – charm
Anachronism – out of time
Analogous – corresponding
Anathema – curse
Anchorite – hermit
Annals – records
Anneal – to toughen
Anomaly – irregularity
Anthropoid – resembling man
Anthropology – science of man
Antithesis – opposite
Antipathy – dislike
Apartheid – racial segregation
Apathetic – indifferent
Apex – peak
Aphorism – proverb
Aplomb – poise
Apocalypse – revelation
Apocryphal – of doubtful authority
Apogee – highest point
Apostasy – renunciation of a faith
Apotheosis – deification
Appal – horrify
Appellation – name
Append – to attach
Apposite – appropriate
Apprise – to give notice
Approbrious – shameful
Arabesque – ornament

Arabesque

Arable – ploughable
Arbiter – judge
Arboreal – living among trees
Archetype – example
Archive – record
Arduous – laborious

Arduous

Arraign – bring before a court
Arrogate – claim without right
Artifice – deception
Ascetic – self denial
Asperity – harshness
Aspersion – slanderous remarks
Assay – attempt
Assiduous – devoted
Assimilate – to absorb
Assuage – to satisfy
Astral – relating to stars
Astute – shrewd

BRICKS THAT BUILD

Athwart – in opposition to
Atrophy – wasting away
Attenuate – dilute
Attrition – rubbing against
Augur – to foretell
Auspices – protection
Austerity – severity
Autonomy – self government
Avarice – greed
Averse – reluctant
Awry – in the wrong direction

Badger – to annoy
Baleful – destructive
Banal – commonplace
Baneful – evil
Banter – good natured ridicule
Baroque – highly ornate
Bastion – fortification
Beguile – to cheat
Bellicose – warlike
Benediction – blessing
Beneficence – charity
Benign – kindly
Bestride – to straddle
Biennial – every two years
Blasphemy – contempt for God
Blatant – noisy
Blithe – joyous
Bluster – to be noisy
Bourgeois – middle class
Broach – introduce
Bromidic – tiresome
Brusque – blunt in manner

Blithe

Bucolic – rustic
Buffoon – clown
Burgeon – sprout
Burnish – polish by rubbing

Cabal – conspiracy
Cache – hiding place
Cacophony – discord
Cadence – rhythm
Caduceus – symbol
Cairn – heap of stones
Caitiff – scoundrels
Cajole – coax
Callow – immature
Calumniate – to slander
Canaille – mob
Cant – *slang* : pretence
Capacious – spacious
Capitulate – surrender
Capricious – whimsical
Captious – fault finding
Carnal – of the body
Carnivorous – flesh eating

Buffoon

Carnivorous

Carrion – decaying flesh
Carte Blanche – unrestricted authority

BRICKS THAT BUILD

Castigate – to criticize
Cataclysm – violent change
Catalyst – substance causing change
Catastrophe – calamity
Catechism – elementary religious book

Catechism

Cathartic – cleansing
Catholic – universal
Causerie – a chat
Caveat – warning
Cavil – find fault
Celibacy – unmarried state
Cerebration – process of thought
Chaff – rubbish
Chagrin – disappointment
Challis – soft cotton fabric
Charlatan – impostor
Charnel – burial place
Charry – careful
Chastisement – zealous patriotism
Chicanery – fraud
Chide – rebuke
Chimerical – imaginary
Churlish – rude
Circumlocution – round about way of writing

Circumspect – watchful
Circumvent – to go around
Citadel – fortress
Cite – to quote
Clairvoyant – foretelling future
Clandestine – secret
Cleave – adhere
Cliche – overworked expression
Climacteric – critical
Coadjutor – helper
Coerce – compel
Cogent – convincing
Cogitate – think
Cognate – related
Cohesion – sticking together
Cohort – company
Collate – to collect in order
Collegiate – belonging to a college
Colloquial – informal conversation
Colloquy – conference

Colloquy

Collusion – secret agreement
Comatose – lethargic
Comity – friendly feeling
Commensurate – equal to
Commiseration – sympathy
Commodious – roomy
Commutation – substitution
Complacent – self satisfied
Compunction – remorse
Conclave – private meeting
Concomitant – accompanying
Concurrent – running together
Condign – well deserved
Condiment – spice
Condole – express sympathy
Condone – to pardon
Conduce – lead to
Confidant – one confided in
Conflagration – big fire
Confute – overwhelm with arguments
Congeal – change from fluid to solid
Congenital – dating from birth
Conglomerate – mixture
Congruent – in agreement
Conjecture – guess
Conjure – produce with magic
Connive – help in wrong doing
Consecrate – to make holy
Consign – transfer
Consonance – agreement
Consort – wife
Consummate – to complete

Contentious

Contentious – quarrelsome
Contingent – conditional
Contravene – oppose
Contrition – repentance
Controvert – to dispute
Contumely – contempt
Conversant – familiar
Convivial – gay
Convoke – to call together
Copious – plentiful
Corporeal – bodily
Corpulent – fat
Corroborate – to confirm
Cortege – procession
Cosmopolitan – belonging to the world
Coterie – small group
Countermand – to revoke an order
Covert – hidden
Covetous – avaricious
Cozen – to cheat
Crag – rock

BRICKS THAT BUILD

Crass – stupid
Craven – cowardly
Credence – belief
Credulous – inclined to believe
Crimp – make wavy
Crux – cross shaped
Cryptic – mysterious
Cudgel – thick stick
Culmination – acme
Culpable – guilty
Cupidity – greed
Cursory – superficial
Cygnet – young swan

Dale – valley
Dalliance – dawdling
Dank – damp
Dappled – marked with spots
Dastard – coward
Dandle – waste time
Dearth – scarcity
Debase – to reduce dignity
Debauch – to corrupt
Debilitate – weaken
Debonair – courteous
Decadence – deterioration
Decant – to pour gently
Deciduous – leaf shedding
Declivity – downward slope
Decorous – proper
Decry – to clamour against
Deduce – to derive by reasoning
Defalcation – embezzlement
Defamation – slander

Deify – to worship as god
Deign – condescend
Deleterious – harmful
Delineate – to mark off
Demagogue – leader who incites
Demur – hesitate
Denizen – inhabitants
Deprecate – belittle
Derelict – abandoned
Descry – spy out
Deterrent – that discourages
Detonate – explode
Diabolic – devilish
Diadem – a crown
Dichotomy – division
Didactic – instructive
Digress – to wander
Dissimilation – disguise
Distraught – bewildered
Docile – easily led
Dogma – system of beliefs
Doleful – sorrowful
Dolorous – dismal

Diadem

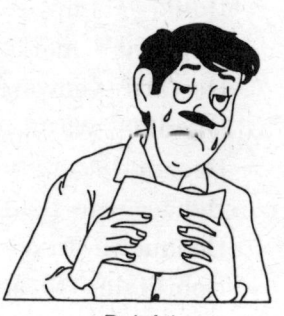
Doleful

Ebullience – boiling up
Ecclesiastical – relating to church
Eclat – brilliant success
Eclectic – selective
Edifice – building
Ecumenical – general
Edict – public notice
Effigy – image
Effulgent – illuminated

Effusive – gushing out
Egress – exit
Elegy – mournful poem
Embellish – adorn
Emulate – to try to equal
Encomium – praise
Ennui – weariness
Enthral – enchant
Equivocate – deceive
Erode – wear away
Erudite – scholarly
Esoteric – secret
Ethereal – spirit like
Ethnic – referring to a race
Eulogy – praise
Euphemism – mild expression
Euphoria – sense of well being
Evoke – call forth
Exhume – to dig out
Existentialism – philosophy of a purposeless world
Excoriate – to skin
Exonerate – free from guilt
Exorbitant – unreasonable
Extirpate – cut out
Extricate – to free

Facetious – humorous
Facile – expert
Fallow – lying idle
Fastidious – difficult to be pleased
Fecund – fertile
Fetid – stinking
Flaccid – not firm

Flagrant – openly disgraceful
Flagitious – wicked
Flaunt – to show off
Florid – flowery

Florid

Flout – to scoff at
Foible – weakness
Foray – plundering raid
Fulminate – to denounce
Fustian – worthless

Gainsay – to deny
Garble – to confuse
Garrulous – talkative
Germane – pertinent
Gibber – talk foolishly
Glib – speak fluently
Gnostic – wise
Goad – urge
Gratuitous – free
Grimace – distort features
Grouse – complain
Guile – deceit
Gyrate – to spin

Haggard – careworn
Halcyon – peaceful
Hallucination – delusion
Harbinger – herald
Hauteur – pride
Hedonist – lover of pleasures
Helix – coil of wire
Heretical – not agreeing
Histrionic – theatrical
Hoary – white because of age
Holocaust – great destruction
Homily – sermon
Horatory – encouraging
Hurtle – rush headlong
Hyperbole – exaggeration
Hypochondria – fallacies of bad health
Hypothesis – assumption

Iconoclast – image breaker
Idiosyncrasy – personal peculiarity
Idyllic – simple, poetic
Ignoble – base
Imbrue – to stain
Impalpable – not evident
Impeach – accuse
Impeccable – faultless
Impede – hinder
Imperceptible – not easily seen
Impervious – not to be penetrated
Importune – to beg
Imprecation – curse
Impugn – to question
Impunity – exemption from punishment

Impute – to blame
Inarticulate – not distinct
Incarcerate – imprison
Incognito – concealed identity
Incubus – burden
Indigent – poor
Indite – write
Indolent – lazy
Indurate – hardened
Inebriated – drunk
Ineffable – indescribable
Inert – sluggish
Inexorable – unyielding
Ingenous – innocent
Ingratiate – to establish in favour
Inquitous – sinful
Innocuous – harmless
Innuendo – insinuation
Insidious – treacherous
Interdict – official order
Intransigent – uncompromising
Introvert – run inward
Inveigh – to attack
Inveterate – firmly established
Invidious – odious
Iterate – repeat
Itinerant – travelling on a circuit

Jaded – worn out
Jargon – confused talk
Jocose – humorous
Juxtaposed – close together

Inebriated

Kith

. **Kith** – friends
Kiosk – stand which is open on one side

Lacerate – to tear
Laconic – brief
Lampoon – satire
Languish – to become weak
Lascivious – lewd
Libel – defamation
Litany – prayer

Litany

Liturgy – religious ritual
Livid – black and blue
Loquacious – talkative
Lucre – riches
Ludicrous – laughable
Lugubrious – sad

Macabre – gruesome
Macerate – to soften by dipping
Magnanimous – generous
Maladroit – clumsy
Malaise – discomfort
Mandate – specific order
Martinet – disciplinarian
Mawkish – nauseating
Medley – mixture
Mellifluent – sweetly flowing
Mendacious – lying
Mendicant – beggar
Meretricious – attractive
Mien – bearing
Militate – operate against
Mitigate – to lessen
Modicum – small quantity
Monolith – a large piece of stone
Mordant – biting
Moribund – lifeless
Motley – miscellaneous
Myriad – many

Mendicant

Nadir – lowest point
Narcissism – love of oneself

Nebulous – hazy
Niggardly – stingy
Nihilism – disbelief in religion
Noxious – harmful

Obdurate – callous
Obeissance – bowing
Obesity – fatness
Oblation – solemn offering
Obloquy – disgrace
Obtrude – to thrust
Obviate – to prevent
Olfactory – pertaining to the sense of smell
Ominous – threatening
Onerous – difficult
Opulence – riches
Ordure – filth
Orifice – opening
Ossify – to become rigid
Ostentatious – pretentious

Paean – song of praise
Palatable – sense of taste
Pall – to become dull
Palliate – to mitigate
Panegyric – eulogy
Panoply – set of armour
Paradigm – model
Paradox – apparently contradictory
Parity – equality
Parochial – provincial
Paroxysm – a fit

Pastoral – pertaining to rural life

Pastoral

Patrimony – inheritance
Pecuniary – financial
Peremptory – positive
Percussion – impact
Penurious – stingy
Perquisite – incidental compensation
Peroration – last part of the speech
Perspicuity – clearness in expression
Pervade – to spread
Perverse – contrary
Philistine – narrow-minded person
Philology – study of words
Picaresque – pertaining to rogues
Piquant – pungent
Plagiarism – stealing ideas
Platitude – trite remark
Plethora – over supply
Polemics – art of disputing
Pontificate – speak like a church priest
Posterity – succeeding generation

Portend – warn

Portend

Pragmatic – practical
Precipitous – steep
Preclude – to prevent
Precursor – predecessor
Predatory – plundering
Predilection – preference
Preposterous – absurd
Prerogative – privilege
Prevaricate – to lie
Pristine – primitive
Probity – integrity
Prodigious – large
Progeny – offspring
Providential – fortunate
Putative – supposed
Putrefy – decay

Qualm – feeling of fear
Quandary – doubt
Query – question
Quirk – turn
Quixotic – visionary

Raillery – banter
Rabid – furious
Rancour – anger

Rancour

Rankle – irritate
Rapacity – greediness
Recalcitrant – stubborn
Reciprocal – in return
Regale – entertain
Relegate – assign
Remission – pardon
Renegade – deserter
Replete – full
Reprisal – injury in return
Repudiate – to refuse
Restitution – compensation
Resurgent – rising again
Retrogression – going back
Revile – to scold
Rudiment – first stage

Sagacious – wise
Salacious – obscene
Saline – salty

BRICKS THAT BUILD

Salubrious – healthful
Salutary – wholesome
Sanguine – confident
Sardonic – ironical
Satiate – satisfy
Saturnine – gloomy
Schism – division
Scruple – reluctance
Sedentary – sluggish
Sedulous – painstaking
Sententious – magisterial
Sentiment – feeling
Sequester – to seclude
Slake – to lessen
Slough – muddy ground
Sojourn – temporary stay
Solicitude – concern
Sophism – fallacy
Specious – deceptive
Splenetic – peevish
Sporadic – occasional
Stigma – blemish
Stilted – elevated
Suave – polite
Sublimate – purify
Subpoena – summons
Subterfuge – false excuse
Succinct – brief
Succour – help
Surreptitious – secret
Surrogate – deputy
Swathe – bind
Sycophant – flatterer

Sentiment

Succour

Taciturn – silent
Talus – slope
Tautology – needless repetition
Temerity – rashness
Thrall – slave
Tiara – head dress
Tirade – strong speech
Tome – volume
Torpor – dullness
Tractable – easily led
Tranquillity – calmness
Transmute – change
Transpire – to become known
Transverse – lying across
Trauma – wound

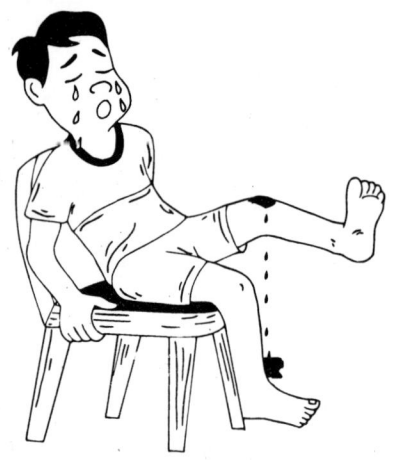

Trauma

Travail – labour pains
Tremulous – shaking
Trepidation – trembling
Tribulation – trouble
Tumid – swollen

Turbulent – violent
Turpitude – shameful depravity
Tutelage – instructions

Ubiquity – omnipresent
Unctuous – oily or smooth
Ungainly – clumsy
Upbraid – to reproach
Uproarious – noisy
Urbane – refined
Uxorious – fond of wife

Vapid – dull
Vacuity – stupidity
Vagary – whim
Vanguard – leader
Variegate – diversify
Vaunt – boast
Vendetta – revenge
Venerate – respect
Verdant – green
Vernal – pertaining to spring

Vernal

Vertigo – dizziness
Viable – capable of living
Vilify – to defame

Vindicate – justify
Vituperate – defame
Vociferous – noisy
Volition – will
Voracious – greedy
Votary – devotee

Votary

Waft – current of wind
Waggery – mischievous merriment

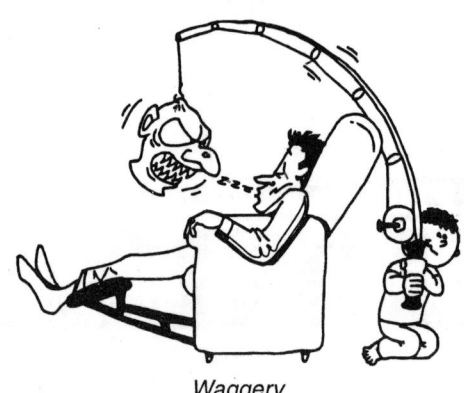

Waggery

Wainscot – wooden panelling
Wean – detach

Welter – roll about
Wheedle – to coax
Wizened – withered
Wont – accustomed
Woof – fabric
Wrath – anger
Wraith – ghost

Wraith

Xylem – woody tissue of plants

Yak – species of ox
Yen – monetary unit

Zany – clown
Zeal – enthusiasm
Zenith – highest point of the sky

Words and Their Opposites in Meaning

Abundance	Scarcity	Deep	Shallow
Acquit	Convict	Deficit	Surplus
Acute	Obtuse	Delay	Growth
Adversity	Prosperity	Deserve	Forfeit
Advisable	Inadvisable	Desist	Persist
Affection	Aversion	Despair	Hope
Agreeable	Disagreeable	Discover	Conceal
Ample	Scanty	Disease	Health
Artful	Straight-forward	Display	Hide, conceal
		Draw	Repel
Artificial	Natural	Dwarf	Giant
Ascent	Descent	Economy	Extravagance
Assemble	Disperse	Enrich	Impoverish
Assent	Dissent	Even	Odd
Barren	Fertile	Flat	Hilly
Bear (carry)	Drop	Foul	Fair
Belief	Disbelief	Gather	Scatter
Beneficial	Injurious	Generous	Selfish
Bitter	Sweet	Gratitude	Ingratitude
Brittle	Tough	Grief	Joy
Bustle	Quiet	Guilty	Innocent
Care	Neglect	Hatred	Love
Cautious	Reckless	Heaven	Hell
Cease	Continue	Hinder	Help
Clever	Stupid	Hollow	Solid
Conclusion	Start	Honesty	Dishonesty
Contrast	Comparison	Honour	Dishonour
Convex	Concave	Humble	Proud
Credit	Debit	Hurt	Heal
Cruel	Kind	Ignorance	Knowledge
Death	Life	Important	Unimportant
Decision	Indecision	Interest	Indifference

BRICKS THAT BUILD

Justice	Injustice	Quarrelsome	Friendly
Lengthen	Shorten	Reap	Sow
Lessen	Augment	Recovery	Relapse
Light	Darkness	Retreat	Advance
Loyal	Disloyal	Rough	Smooth
Make	Mar	Satisfy	Dissatisfy
Master	Servant	Seldom	Often
Mild	Harsh	Strange	Familiar
Miser	Spendthrift	Summit	Base
Motion	Rest	Teach	learn
Natural	Artificial	Top	Bottom
Optimist	Pessimist	Transparent	Opaque
Ordinary	Extra-ordinary	Truth	Falsehood
		Urban	Rural
Permit	Prohibit	Urgent	Unimportant
Pleasant	Unpleasant	Usual	Unusual
Pleasure	Pain	Vague	Definite
Plenty	Scarce	Vertical	Horizontal
Polite	Proud	Virtue	Vice
Positive	Negative	Voluntary	Compulsory
Pride	Humility	Weary	Fresh
Pure	Mixed	Wild	Tame

For Assimilation
UNIT 1

Directions. *Each of the numbered words given below* is *followed by four lettered words. For each numbered word select the lettered word which is closest in meaning.*

1. **Lethal**
   - (a) deadly
   - (b) sluggish
   - (c) smooth
   - (d) unlawful
2. **Limpid**
   - (a) moist
   - (b) dear
   - (c) drooping
   - (d) flimsy

3. **Machination**
   - (a) labour-saving
   - (b) evil plot
   - (c) factory work
   - (d) engine part
4. **Malingering**
   - (a) creating ill-will
   - (b) feigning illness
   - (c) defaming
   - (d) being habitually lazy
5. **Melee**
   - (a) kindness
   - (b) brawl
   - (c) simple song
   - (d) primitive dance
6. **Molecule**
   - (a) little heap of earth
   - (b) birthmark
   - (c) enormous
   - (d) particle
7. **Nautical**
   - (a) perverse
   - (b) disgusting
   - (c) naval
   - (d) unaffected
8. **Nostalgia**
   - (a) aroma
   - (b) sea-sickness
   - (c) homesickness
   - (d) cure-all
9. **Obtuse**
   - (a) difficult
   - (b) interfering
   - (c) blunt
   - (d) concealed
10. **Omnipotent**
    - (a) all-knowing
    - (b) all powerful
    - (c) everlasting
    - (d) all merciful
11. **Orientation**
    - (a) eastward migration
    - (b) adherence to Asiatic customs
    - (c) adjustment to facts
    - (d) teaching new theories
12. **Ostensibly**
    - (a) actually
    - (b) conspicuously
    - (c) apparently
    - (d) quietly

13. **Ostentatious**
    - (a) protruding
    - (b) wealthy
    - (c) decorative
    - (d) showy
14. **Panorama**
    - (a) broad scene
    - (b) ancient Grecian temple
    - (c) light-weight hat
    - (d) pretty
15. **Penitence**
    - (a) retribution
    - (b) submission
    - (c) confinement
    - (d) repentance
16. **Mystical**
    - (a) imaginary
    - (b) vague
    - (c) prophetic
    - (d) spiritually symbolic
17. **Singular**
    - (a) extraordinary
    - (b) simple
    - (c) to the point
    - (d) representative
18. **Infallible**
    - (a) outspoken
    - (b) weak
    - (c) authentic
    - (d) unerring
19. **Enigmatic**
    - (a) pithy
    - (b) puzzling
    - (c) complicated
    - (d) illusive
20. **Dogged**
    - (a) agile
    - (b) persistent
    - (c) awkward
    - (d) ill-starred
21. **Improvident**
    - (a) thriftless
    - (b) Incautious
    - (c) unhappy
    - (d) shabby
22. **Adept**
    - (a) versatile
    - (b) skilful
    - (c) smart
    - (d) effortless

23. **Turbulent**
    - (a) savage
    - (b) uncontrollable
    - (c) agitated
    - (d) dull
24. **Steadfast**
    - (a) strong
    - (b) constant
    - (c) slow but sure
    - (d) dull
25. **Wily**
    - (a) crafty
    - (b) evasive
    - (c) humorous
    - (d) dishonest
26. **Cordial**
    - (a) smooth
    - (b) friendly
    - (c) sophisticated
    - (d) reserved
27. **Voluble**
    - (a) fat
    - (b) loud
    - (c) talkative
    - (d) rambling
28. **Fallacious**
    - (a) quarrelsome
    - (b) superficial
    - (c) vindictive
    - (d) deceptive
29. **Inextricable**
    - (a) unexplainable
    - (b) firm
    - (c) unsolvable
    - (d) inessential
30. **Evocative**
    - (a) noisy
    - (b) plausible
    - (c) exact
    - (d) arousing memories
31. **Impassioned**
    - (a) ardent
    - (b) earnest
    - (c) enarmoured
    - (d) haughty
32. **Provisional**
    - (a) casual
    - (b) lucky
    - (c) visible
    - (d) temporary
33. **Indignity**
    - (a) penalty
    - (b) humiliation
    - (c) blame
    - (d) rebuke

34. **Abstract**
    (a) theoretical
    (b) confused
    (c) indefinite
    (d) unrealistic
35. **Brackish**
    (a) backward
    (b) having a foul smell
    (c) salty
    (d) woody
36. **Heyday**
    (a) excitement
    (b) special event
    (c) comedy
    (d) peak period
37. **Efface**
    (a) to degrade
    (b) erase
    (c) mar
    (d) amid
38. **Cerebral**
    (a) formal
    (b) perceptive
    (c) impressionable
    (d) relating to the brain
39. **Solecism**
    (a) plausible but fallacious argument
    (b) grammatical error
    (c) wise saying
    (d) comfort
40. **Nonentity**
    (a) trifle
    (b) mystical being
    (c) insignificant person
    (d) minor
41. **Succulent**
    (a) greedy
    (b) tasty
    (c) juicy
    (d) soft
42. **Musty**
    (a) mouldy
    (b) gloomy
    (c) acrid
    (d) grubby
43. **Itinerant**
    (a) irregular
    (b) temporary
    (c) poor
    (d) travelling

44. **Defray**
    (a) to pay
    (b) pull back
    (c) tatter
    (d) go round
45. **Medallion**
    (a) souvenir
    (b) precious metal
    (c) religious relic
    (d) large medal
46. **Duplicity**
    (a) repetition
    (b) artlessness
    (c) double-dealing
    (d) cleverness
47. **Caricature**
    (a) biographical sketch
    (b) grotesque likeness
    (c) eccentricity
    (d) personality trait
48. **Heinous**
    (a) abominable
    (b) obscure
    (c) reasonable
    (d) ugly
49. **Emit**
    (a) to keep out
    (b) give off
    (c) acknowledge
    (d) let in
50. **Fettle**
    (a) condition
    (b) shackle
    (c) humour
    (d) problem
51. **Lineage**
    (a) chain of command
    (b) prestige
    (c) ancestry
    (d) rigging
52. **Undue**
    (a) undisciplined
    (b) usurious
    (c) premature
    (d) unjustified
53. **Militate**
    (a) to make less severe
    (b) challenge
    (c) have weight
    (d) arbitrate or influence

BRICKS THAT BUILD 121

54. **Extol**
    - (a) to flatter
    - (b) acknowledge
    - (c) deprive of
    - (d) praise

55. **Substantiate**
    - (a) to confirm
    - (b) indicate
    - (c) substitute
    - (d) emphasize

56. **Badger**
    - (a) to beat
    - (b) pester
    - (c) dig into
    - (d) exhaust

57. **Cavil**
    - (a) to find fault
    - (b) ridicule
    - (c) dissemble
    - (d) humble onset

58. **Subvert**
    - (a) to replace
    - (b) divide
    - (c) sink
    - (d) overthrow

59. **Jeopardise**
    - (a) to unbalance
    - (b) wear way
    - (c) endanger
    - (d) belittle

60. **Commandeer**
    - (a) to commit
    - (b) to take possession of
    - (c) destroy
    - (d) redirect

61. **Exhort**
    - (a) to urge
    - (b) try hard
    - (c) tamper with
    - (d) shake down

62. **Mollify**
    - (a) to deny
    - (b) change
    - (c) pacify
    - (d) subdue

63. **Brandish**
    - (a) to bum into
    - (b) browbeat
    - (c) torment
    - (d) wave threateningly

For Assimilation
UNIT 2

Directions. *In each of the following questions, one word* in *bold letters* is *followed by four or five words or expressions. Choose the word or expression that has most nearly the opposite meaning of the word* in *the words in responses. Mark the word as the answer to the question.*

1. **Profusion**
   - (a) travesty
   - (b) validity
   - (c) scarcity
   - (d) ordinance
   - (e) laudanum

2. **Agnostic**
   - (a) aged
   - (b) fanatic
   - (c) truncated
   - (d) productive
   - (e) inebriate

3. **Mitigation**
   - (a) aggravation
   - (b) verdancy
   - (c) obscenity
   - (d) restriction
   - (e) interregnum

4. **Misanthropic**
   - (a) angelic
   - (b) hypnotised
   - (c) supercilious
   - (d) biologic
   - (e) humanitarian

5. **Iniquity**
   - (a) equity
   - (b) rectitude
   - (c) peace
   - (d) apostasy
   - (e) calmness

6. **Protuberance**
   - (a) cadence
   - (b) habitation
   - (c) indentation
   - (d) appendage
   - (e) timbrel

BRICKS THAT BUILD

7. **Ingenuous**
   - (a) genuflecting
   - (b) hypothetical
   - (c) spasmodic
   - (d) genuine
   - (e) hypocritical

8. **Sanctimonious**
   - (a) contumacious
   - (b) flagitious
   - (c) zany
   - (d) ingenuous
   - (e) impervious

9. **Extirpate**
   - (a) propagate
   - (b) inseminate
   - (c) ingratiate
   - (d) emasculate
   - (e) daub

10. **Ameliorate**
    - (a) to better
    - (b) dissemble
    - (c) spoil
    - (d) clasp

11. **Abridge**
    - (a) augment
    - (b) subdue
    - (c) encourage
    - (d) elaborate

12. **Aversion**
    - (a) affinity
    - (b) amnesty
    - (c) playful
    - (d) augury

13. **Assuage**
    - (a) detest
    - (b) provoke
    - (c) wrap
    - (d) mislead

14. **Cajole**
    - (a) synthesize
    - (b) antagonize
    - (c) assimilate
    - (d) proper

15. **Venerate**
    - (a) abominate
    - (b) adapt
    - (c) correlate
    - (d) involve

16. **Sycophancy**
    - (a) frankness
    - (b) explain
    - (c) wicked
    - (d) covetous

17. **Inaugurate**
    - (a) facilitate
    - (b) inculcate
    - (c) terminate
    - (d) gesticulate
18. **Dubious**
    - (a) sure
    - (b) pathetic
    - (c) impotence
    - (d) idiom
19. **Enervate**
    - (a) introduce
    - (b) debilitate
    - (c) conclude
    - (d) fortify
20. **Magnify**
    - (a) produce
    - (b) support
    - (c) reduce
    - (d) destroy
21. **Optimistic**
    - (a) gloomy
    - (b) cynic
    - (c) sadist
    - (d) pessimistic
22. **Rejoice**
    - (a) excite
    - (b) cite
    - (c) lament
    - (d) bright
23. **Retreat**
    - (a) lett
    - (b) liberalize
    - (c) advance
    - (d) more
24. **Resolve**
    - (a) involve
    - (b) unstable
    - (c) hesitate
    - (d) decide
25. **Steadfast**
    - (a) weak
    - (b) unstable
    - (c) wavering
    - (d) linger
26. **Shallow**
    - (a) narrow
    - (b) wide
    - (c) deep
    - (d) low
27. **Strange**
    - (a) unusual
    - (b) familiar
    - (c) common
    - (d) ordinary

BRICKS THAT BUILD

28. **Scarce**
    - (a) shortage
    - (b) abundance
    - (c) lavish
    - (d) superfluous

29. **Praise**
    - (a) deny
    - (b) silent
    - (c) criticize
    - (d) condemn

30. **Attract**
    - (a) drive
    - (b) expel
    - (c) repel
    - (d) demote

31. **Build**
    - (a) destroy
    - (b) demolish
    - (c) construct
    - (d) rear up

32. **Bulky**
    - (a) substantial
    - (b) unwieldy
    - (c) short
    - (d) thin

33. **Careful**
    - (a) cautious
    - (b) negligent
    - (c) negligible
    - (d) important

34. **Minimise**
    - (a) endanger
    - (b) itemise
    - (c) demolish
    - (d) expand
    - (e) distribute

35. **Emissary**
    - (a) spy
    - (b) receptionist
    - (c) protector
    - (d) scribe
    - (e) dictator

36. **Premonition**
    - (a) dangerous action
    - (b) complete surprise
    - (c) later action
    - (d) unusual suggestion
    - (e) heartly congratulations

37. **Monotonous**
    (a) incomprehensible
    (b) newly discovered
    (c) exciting
    (d) acceptable
    (e) difficult
38. **Multitude**
    (a) handful
    (b) majority
    (c) minority
    (d) quorum
    (e) crowd
39. **Misanthrope**
    (a) philanthropist
    (b) victim
    (c) vandal
    (d) miser
    (e) soldier
40. **Nominal**
    (a) valuable
    (b) sworn
    (c) fictitious
    (d) believable
    (e) actual
41. **Innovate**
    (a) sell
    (b) buy
    (c) choose
    (d) copy
    (e) own
42. **Omnipotent**
    (a) safe
    (b) strong
    (c) good
    (d) weak
    (e) sour
43. **Rhetoric**
    (a) lack of knowledge
    (b) fear of learning
    (c) abuse of language
    (d) attempt at telling
    (e) reason for knowing
44. **Obdurate**
    (a) hard-headed
    (b) quick-witted
    (c) sharp-eyed
    (d) soft-hearted
    (e) heavy-handed

BRICKS THAT BUILD

45. **Neophyte**
    (a) professional (b) veteran
    (c) student (d) clown
    (e) pilot

46. **Noncombatant**
    (a) fighter (b) coward
    (c) judge (d) loser
    (e) arbitrator

47. **Minority**
    (a) democratic victory (b) successful crowd
    (c) winning group (d) wisest men
    (e) largest number

48. **Admonish**
    (a) scold (b) honour
    (c) encourage (d) remember
    (e) understand

49. **Monologue**
    (a) solo (b) novel
    (c) pantomime (d) conversation
    (e) speech

50. **Multilateral**
    (a) unequal (b) one-sided
    (c) preplanned (d) overeager
    (e) single-answered

51. **Pacify**
    (a) end disagreement (b) begin new methods
    (c) stir up anger (d) try quietly
    (e) solve illegally

52. **Pedagogue**
    (a) doctor (b) loser
    (c) winner (d) student
    (e) leader

53. **Pensive**
    (a) thoughtless
    (b) careless
    (c) eager
    (d) penitent
    (e) unattached
54. **Euphony**
    (a) lively music
    (b) harsh sound
    (c) dull arrangement
    (d) loud volume
    (e) fast rhythm
55. **Dispossess**
    (a) remove completely
    (b) try saving
    (c) help inhabit
    (d) give generously
    (e) omit willingly
56. **Deport**
    (a) bring in
    (b) try out
    (c) secure
    (d) give in
    (e) intend
57. **Postlude**
    (a) adenda
    (b) theme
    (c) orchestration
    (d) overture
    (e) harmony
58. **Potent**
    (a) prepared
    (b) lost
    (c) quality
    (d) ready
    (e) weak
59. **Polygon**
    (a) small building
    (b) equal sides
    (c) uneven length
    (d) straight line
    (e) soft corner
60. **Pervert**
    (a) prophesy
    (b) glorify
    (c) deceive
    (d) abuse
    (e) purify

61. Apathy
   (a) sleep
   (b) temptation
   (c) zeal
   (d) hospitality
   (e) immaturity

62. Panacea
   (a) blessing
   (b) poison
   (c) triumph
   (d) plunder
   (e) confinement

63. Paraphrase
   (a) act
   (b) sing
   (c) quote
   (d) demand
   (e) qualify

64. Compulsion
   (a) illegitimacy
   (b) improvement
   (c) significance
   (d) indifference
   (e) confinement

65. Polygamy
   (a) monogamy
   (b) friendship
   (c) morality
   (d) humanity
   (e) bachelorhood

66. Abdicate
   (a) seize
   (b) speak softly
   (c) crown
   (d) give out
   (e) obey

67. Component
   (a) hoard
   (b) total
   (c) foundation
   (d) legend
   (e) part

68. Prime
   (a) uneven
   (b) worst
   (c) correct
   (d) slight
   (e) destroyed

69. **Sedentary**
    (a) nomadic
    (b) multiple
    (c) original
    (d) fearsome
    (e) repairable
70. **Sentimental**
    (a) unwilling
    (b) unequal
    (c) unreliable
    (d) unpardonable
    (e) unresponsive
71. **Consequence**
    (a) trial
    (b) plan
    (c) cause
    (d) retaliation
    (e) curiosity
72. **Absolve**
    (a) free
    (b) struggle
    (c) accuse
    (d) cheat
    (e) testify
73. **Circumspect**
    (a) eager
    (b) careless
    (c) cautious
    (d) quarrelsome
    (e) guiding
74. **Inspire**
    (a) intend
    (b) pretend
    (c) exchange
    (d) outline
    (e) discourage
75. **Constrict**
    (a) loosen
    (b) repeat
    (c) inspect
    (d) destroy
    (e) impress
76. **Subterfuge**
    (a) righteousness
    (b) honesty
    (c) prudence
    (d) respect
    (e) cloudiness

BRICKS THAT BUILD 131

77. **Superb**
    (a) terrible
    (b) unknown
    (c) common
    (d) expanded
    (e) wasted

78. **Synchronized**
    (a) out of place
    (b) out of time
    (c) out of breath
    (d) out of luck

79. **Derogatory**
    (a) uneven
    (b) equal
    (c) opposite
    (d) flattering
    (e) victorious

80. **Prescribe**
    (a) misunderstand
    (b) ministerial
    (c) misconduct
    (d) misspend
    (e) misdirect

81. **Consent**
    (a) obey
    (b) disagree
    (c) hate
    (d) retire
    (e) explain

82. **Tangible**
    (a) required
    (b) explainable
    (c) presentable
    (d) illegal
    (e) untouchable

83. **Tenacity**
    (a) safety
    (b) individual
    (c) smallness
    (d) surrender
    (e) pleasure

84. **Wane**
    (a) pane
    (b) wax
    (c) warn
    (d) weave

85. **Conceal**
    (a) tell
    (b) think
    (c) reveal
    (d) deal

86. **Animosity**
    (a) thoughtfulness (b) eagerness
    (c) reliability (d) anxiety
    (e) friendliness
87. **Acrimonious**
    (a) sprightly (b) intelligent
    (c) soothing (d) bitter
    (e) plain
88. **Philanthropy**
    (a) inhumanity (b) beneficence
    (c) argument (d) waste
    (e) science
89. **Antipathy**
    (a) joyfulness (b) attraction
    (c) hatred (d) unwillingness
    (e) protest
90. **Benefactor**
    (a) helper (b) victor
    (c) enemy (d) disciple
    (e) teacher
91. **Belligerent**
    (a) loud (b) interested
    (c) popular (d) peaceful
    (e) colourful
92. **Avert**
    (a) hide (b) obey
    (c) excuse (d) deny
    (e) cause
93. **Autocratic**
    (a) independent (b) cooperative
    (c) kind (d) inspirational
    (e) charitable

BRICKS THAT BUILD

94. **Antecedent**
    (a) offspring
    (b) relative
    (c) improvement
    (d) willingness
    (e) explanation

95. **Amicable**
    (a) wise
    (b) believable
    (c) friendly
    (d) sullen
    (e) eager

96. **Ambidextrous**
    (a) clumsy
    (b) helpful
    (c) composed
    (d) independent
    (e) high-handed

97. **Magnanimous**
    (a) generous
    (b) conscious
    (c) petty
    (d) reliable
    (e) purposeful

98. **Archetype**
    (a) print
    (b) origin
    (c) factory
    (d) copy
    (e) lesson

99. **Inaudible**
    (a) felt
    (b) resonant
    (c) expansive
    (d) opportune
    (e) straided

ANSWERS
Unit-I

1. (a) 2. (c) 3. (b) 4. (a) 5. (b) 6. (d)
7. (c) 8. (c) 9. (c) 10. (b) 11. (c) 12. (c)
13. (d) 14. (a) 15. (d) 16. (d) 17. (a) 18. (d)
19. (b) 20. (b) 21. (b) 22. (b) 23. (c) 24. (b)
25. (a) 26. (b) 27. (c) 28. (d) 29. (a) 30. (d)
31. (a) 32. (d) 33. (b) 34. (d) 35. (c) 36. (d)

37. (b)	38. (d)	39. (b)	40. (c)	41. (c)	42. (c)
43. (d)	44. (a)	45. (a)	46. (c)	47. (b)	48. (a)
49. (b)	50. (a)	51. (c)	52. (d)	53. (b)	54. (d)
55. (a)	56. (b)	57. (a)	58. (d)	59. (c)	60. (b)
61. (a)	62. (c)	63. (d)			

Unit-II

1. (c)	2. (b)	3. (a)	4. (e)	5. (a)	6. (c)
7. (e)	8. (d)	9. (a)	10. (c)	11. (d)	12. (a)
13. (b)	14. (b)	15. (a)	16. (a)	17. (c)	18. (a)
19. (b)	20. (c)	21. (d)	22. (c)	23. (c)	24. (c)
25. (c)	26. (c)	27. (c)	28. (b)	29. (d)	30. (c)
31. (b)	32. (d)	33. (b)	34. (d)	35. (a)	36. (c)
37. (c)	38. (c)	39. (a)	40. (a)	41. (d)	42. (d)
43. (d)	44. (d)	45. (b)	46. (a)	47. (e)	48. (c)
49. (d)	50. (b)	51. (c)	52. (d)	53. (a)	54. (b)
55. (d)	56. (a)	57. (d)	58. (e)	59. (d)	60. (e)
61. (c)	62. (b)	63. (c)	64. (d)	65. (a)	66. (a)
67. (b)	68. (d)	69. (a)	70. (a)	71. (c)	72. (c)
73. (b)	74. (e)	75. (a)	76. (b)	77. (c)	78. (b)
79. (d)	80. (e)	81. (b)	82. (e)	83. (d)	84. (b)
85. (c)	86. (e)	87. (c)	88. (a)	89. (b)	90. (c)
91. (d)	92. (e)	93. (c)	94. (a)	95. (d)	96. (a)
97. (c)	98. (d)	99. (b)			

6

How to Improve Your Writing Power-1
(DESCRIPTIONS)

Whether you are writing a story or a novel or a letter or about a scene, the effectiveness of your writing depends on descriptions. Descriptions beautify a narrative. If a writer gives just a sequence of incidents, it may become boring to a reader. The writer should stop and give a description of some or the other thing. Suppose you are writing a composition on "Journey by train" and you narrate the incidents thus—

> I reached the station in a taxi at 4 p.m. I had had my seat reserved a few days ago. I occupied my seat and the train started on time...

It is uninteresting and boring; a reader will go through it, if he is bound by duty to do so. It is not an effective or impressive narrative. The writer passes on the information to the reader without making it to sink in his mind or to get involved in his thinking process. Had it been interspersed with descriptions, it would have a great appeal. A few sentences of the above given narrative can be made effective with descriptions in the following manner—

> I rushed to the platform as I reached the station on time. To avoid delay, I walked briskly in a zig zag manner gently pushing a few and being gently pushed by a few. Tucking

my luggage on the shelf, I took my seat. I cast a hasty glance at the others sitting beside me and around me. Down-cast eyes of a newly married girl, the withered face of an old woman, a mother fondling her child, a man dusting his shoes and another looking vacantly here and there occupied my mind before the train started...

Detailed descriptions would have been on obstruction in the flow of the narrative. In such cases descriptions should be crisp, brief and effective. The reader with these descriptions will be transported, on the wings of imagination, to that place and time.

Some writers give descriptions even in argumentative piece of writing. It is a difficult job because the descriptions may blunt the argument or break the chain of reasoning or may even divert the attention of the reader. So, only an adept writer can do it. *For example*, Mr. Winston Churchill, while paying a rich tribute to the women in playing an important role in the Second World War says—

This war effort could not have been achieved if the women had not marched forward in millions and undertaken all kinds of tasks and works which any other generation but our own — unless you go back to the Stone Age... would have considered them unfit; work in the fields, heavy work in the foundries and in the shops, very refined work on radio and precision instruments, work in the hospitals, responsible clerical work of all kinds, work throughout the munitions factories, work in the mixed batteries....

Clearly, in the above-quoted passage, Churchill wanted to tell that women's role was very important in multifarious activities. The first sentence up to " them unfit", states a fact and the latter part is the description of the different types of work. The description conveys the correct impression of the vastness of work and makes the phrase "all work" more graphic and conceivable. Such a description should generally be employed as a technique in argumentative speeches. Why should it be so? The audience cannot be attentive all the time; their attention is sure to go astray and such a description serves the purpose of declamation.

How to give descriptions ?

Descriptions are given in a variety of ways

    (i) By picking up significant aspects or details

    (ii) By breaking up a word into its constituents

    (iii) By giving examples and illustrations

    (iv) By making use of metaphors and similes

Picking significant details. No description can be effective if you give all the details without picking and choosing the significant ones. If you are describing *Cricket fever*, you will have to describe its impact on the young children, on shopkeepers, on bus passengers, on house wives etc. We have selected these sections of society by keeping in mind the (a) interest they take in cricket and (b) its impact on their work. Then we pick up significant incidents which show cricket fever interfering with their work. In the case of the young children, we will pick up incidents like (a) they stop and ask everyone listening to the commentary "What is the score, Uncle", (b) they carry transistors in their pockets and switch on it in the class room itself though at a low volume, (c) they get leave from the school and remain glued to the chair in front of the T.V., (d) they jump at a sixer and become crest fallen when a favourite player of theirs is out at a low score, (e) they make movements with their hands simultating bowling or batting in their drawing room, (f) they indulge in heated discussions about the match with their friends, comment on batting or bowling.

If we do not pick up these details, we cannot build up a complete picture with some points sinking in the reader's mind. These details should not be fictitious because purely imaginative description cannot elicit our faith. Descriptions should by real or near reality, otherwise they lack appeal.

Suppose you are writing a composition on "Indian birds". You will have to pick up significant details of their physical features. Only such physical features as may by contrasted with other birds should be taken up. Following is an example of a fine description.

Example

> The complexion of this person was dark, and his age somewhat advanced. He wore his own hair, combed smooth down, and cut very short. It was jet black, slightly curled by nature, and already mottled with grey. The man's features expressed rather knavery than vice, and a disposition to sharpness, cunning, and roguery, more than the traces of stormy and indulged passions. His sharp, quick, black eyes, acute features, ready, sardonic smile, promptitude, and effrontery, gave him altogether what is called among the vulgar a knowing look, which generally implies a tendency to knavery. At a fair or market you could not for a moment have doubted that he was a horse jockey, intimate with all the tricks of his trade; yet had you met him on a moor, you would not have apprehended any violence from him. His dress was also that of a horse-dealer — a close-buttoned jockey-coat, or wrap rascal, as it was then termed, with huge metal buttons, coarse blue upper stockings, called boot-hose, because supplying the place of boots, and a slouched hat. He only wanted a loaded whip under his arm and a spur upon one heel, to complete the dress of the character he seemed to represent.

Comments. The description of the features of the person is very graphic and detailed. About his hair he uses phrases like "jet black", "curled by nature" "mottled with grey" "combed smooth", "cut very short." All these studied in conjunction give us a complete idea about his hair. His eyes have also been described with scientific accuracy — "sharp", "quick" and "black".

In descriptions, contrasts are very important; many a time, these are given with the help of analogies. The writer says that his "dress was that of a horse dealer — a close buttoned jockey coat or wrap rascal... with huge metal buttons, coarse blue upper stocking...". He takes the comparison further by contrasting the man and the horse dealer thus: "He only wanted a loaded whip under his arm and a spur upon one heel..."

> He *was introduced into the Council* Chamber, *as the place is called where the magistrates hold their sittings, and which was then at a little distance from the prison. It was a large room, partially and imperfectly lighted; but by chance, or the skill of the architect, who might happen to remember the advantage which might occasionally be derived from such an arrangement, one window was so placed as to throw a strong light at the foot of the table at which prisoners were usually posted for examination, while the upper end, where the examinants sat, was thrown into shadow.*

Comments. It is the description of a room, particularly with regard to light. The room was dimly lighted. Instead of showing the effect of dim light on different objects — a method which may generally be adopted by a writer of descriptions — he uses the method of elaboration with the help of comments. *For example*: while talking about the window which admitted strong light, he comments by saying that a window was there "by chance or by the skill of the architect who might happen to remember the advantage which might occasionally be derived from such an arrangement". The point has been vividly brought home.

7

How to Improve Your Writing Power-2
(NARRATION)

When you are telling about your experiences of travelling by bus or of attending a class or of meeting an old friend or of telling a lie, you need the skill to narrate. If you are telling the story of a film or giving impressions of a cricket match or an account of a quarrel, you need the power of narrating incidents. Bold narration is not enough. If only a chronological account of incidents in their natural sequence is given, it will be uninteresting and unimpressive. In such a narrative only those who are directly involved in the happenings may be interested. Whether you are a story-teller or a novelist or a commentator or even a common man, you will have to make your narrative interesting. No letter-writer, no biographer and no news-writer can ignore the essential qualities of a good narrative.

Essentials of Good Narraitve

A good narrative must communicate the sequence of incidents in a manner that the listener or the reader takes interest. Only an *Ancient Mariner* (hero of Coleridge's poem) can compel the listener, by hypnotising him, to listen to his story.

In the famous short story entitled. **The Story Teller** the writer tells that the grand mother could not hold the attention of the mischievous children while travelling by train by telling a story. The old woman blamed the children for being inattentive and uncivilised. In fact, the children were asking questions and the grandmother did not answer those questions. A co-passenger told the same story to the same children by giving replies to all the questions of the children. Many times, the replies were ridiculous but the narrator's aim was just to satisfy their curiosity. *For example* at one place the children asked him "Why did the pigs frequent the king's garden ? and he replied to eat flowers." As you know, pigs eat the dirtiest things but the reply of the story-teller was to satisfy the curiosity of the children even if the reply is ridiculous. This is the case with a story but all good narratives have some requisites. These essentials are—

1. chronological order of incidents
2. should be interspersed with descriptions
3. should arouse curiosity
4. incidents should be logically connected
5. should involve the readers or listeners emotionally
6. should have imaginative touches.

Chronological order of incidents

We should not change the order of incidents; we should retain their natural sequence. If the order is changed, the reader's imagination will have to move backward and forward which interferes with his logical thinking. Every incident creates a mood of expectation and the reader wants it to be satisfied. Our logical sense makes us to expect something. It may happen according to our expectations or contrary to them. In the former case we are satisfied whereas in the latter case we are depressed or surprised. Thus, the reader or listener is emotionally involved. If a writer or narrator succeeds in achieving this aim, he is a good narrator.

If the last incident of a sequence of incidents is given in the beginning, the interest of the reader or listener will die. Man, howsoever civilised or matured he may be, has the childish nature of being curious. In the case of a story, a man is quite curious to know its ending and if it is unfolded by stages, his interest remains alive. The reader goes on asking "What next ?" at every incident in a story. This is the main reason of the popularity of detective novels in which a lot of suspense is kept up.

Moreover, chronological order of incidents makes us aware of time also. Certain incidents can be understood better if studied in the context of their time-period.

Should be interspersed with descriptions

If incidents are narrated one after another, it becomes a video film of the happenings. It is not a proper narrative. The writer must momentarily stop the narrative and look around the place where the incident in the story occurs. He should describe something. Such descriptions will make the narrative lively. If the incidents occur at a fast speed, mind cannot keep pace and the reader feels bored. The descriptions make the mind of the reader to take rest and thus refresh itself. If the story is unfolded rapidly, the interest of the reader dies.

Should have suspense

A story without an element of suspense makes it dull. We do not involve ourselves in the story. The reader should go on asking "What next?" "What next ?" In other words, if he comes to know about the last incident right in the beginning, his interest will be lost.

Incidents should be logically connected

If the incidents are unrelated, there will be no development of the story. Digressions, many a time, break the narrative and the interest of the reader comes to an end. The reader loses the thread of the story and is lost in the digressions. Deviations give a jolt to our imagination. The effect built up with the help of the incidents will wither away. So the incidents in a narrative must be in the form of a chain. Every incident must lean back upon the previous one and must lead to the following one. As far as possible, the relationship should be of cause and effect. *For example:* if we say "He failed so he gave up studies" the two incidents (i) failing (ii) giving up studies are cause and effect.

Should involve emotionally

Unless the reader identifies himself with the main character and unless he weeps when the main characters suffer and enjoys when the characters are happy, the story does not serve the purpose. Emotional involvement in the case of a narrative is of utmost significance. This does not mean that a reader becomes sad if he reads a tragic story. Tragedy elevates instead of making us depressed. Aristotle pointed out that tragedy by arousing tragic feelings purges the emotions which are aroused by the tragedy. This process ennobles the thinking of man and leaves the mind healthy.

Should have imaginative touches

Comparisons, parallels and flights of imagination beautify the narrative. The descriptions may be imaginative or comments may be so. *For example :*

> "We reached the edge of the road where stood an oak tree. It was ten times as thick and twice as tall as the birch tree around it. It was enormous, double of a man's span, with ancient scars with huge limbs sprawling with gnarled hands and fingers. It looked like an aged monster angry and scornful among the smiling birch trees. This oak, refuses to yield to the season's spell spurning both spring and sunshine."

The opening sentence of the above given paragraph is in the form of narration — "we reached ...... oak tree" — telling us about an incident. It is followed by descriptions. Imaginative touches are given when he talks of "huge limbs sprawling with an ...... aged monster ......". These touches beautify the description and makes the narrative interesting.

Examples of Narrative Writing

PASSAGE I

These growing charms, in all their juvenile profusion, had no power to shake the steadfast mind, or divert the fixed gaze of the constant Laird of Dumbiedikes. But there was scarce another eye that could behold this living picture of health and beauty, without pausing on it with pleasure. The traveller stopped his weary horse on the eve of entering the city which was the end of his journey, to gaze at the sylph-like form that tripped by him, with her milk-pail poised on her head, bearing herself so erect, and stepping so light and free under her burden, that it seemed rather an ornament than an encumbrance. The lads of the neighbouring suburb, who held their evening rendezvous for putting the stone, casting the hammer, playing at long bowls, and other athletic exercises, watched the motions of Effie Deans, and contended with each other which should have the good fortune to attract her attention. Even the rigid Presbyterians of her father's persuasion, who held each indulgence of the eye and sense to be a snare at least, if not a crime, were surprised into a moment's delight while gazing on a creature so exquisite — instantly checked by a sigh, reproaching at once their own weakness, and mourning that a creature so fair should share in the common and hereditary guilt and imperfection of our nature. She was currently entitled the Lily of St. Leonard's, a name which she deserved as much by her guileless purity of thought, speech and action, as by her uncommon loveliness of face and person.

Comments. No narration can be effective and good till it is punctuated with descriptions. These are only a few incidents — stopping of the tired horse, gazing at the girl, playing children watching Effie Deans etc. but narration of every incident is preceded by the description. The description of the girl: "... the sylph like form that tripped by him with her milk pail poised on her head, bearing herself so erect and stepping so light and free under her burden that it seemed rather an ornament than an encumbrance" is beautiful and justifies the gaze of the people.

This is all right in a novel but in short pieces of composition, description should not be very long. Descriptions break the flow of the narrative but make it more vivid. Simple narration of facts or incidents may be the aim of a scientist but not of a writer.

PASSAGE 2

A lover's hope resembles the bean in the nursery tale—let it once take root, and it will grow so rapidly, that in the course of a few hours the giant Imagination builds a castle on the top, and by and by comes Disappointment with the 'curtal axe, 'and hews down both the plant and the superstructure. Jeanie's fancy, though not the most powerful of her faculties, was lively enough to transport her to a wild farm in Northumberland, well stocked with milk-cows, yeald beasts, and sheep; a meeting — house hard by, frequented by serious Presbyterians, who had united in a harmonious call to Reuben Butler to be their spiritual guide; Effie restored, not to gaiety, but to cheerfulness at least; their father, with his gray hair smoothed down, and spectacles on his nose; herself, with the maiden snood exchanged for a matron's curch — all arranged in a pew in the said meeting-house, listening to words of devotion, rendered sweeter and more powerful by the affectionate ties which combined them with the preacher. She cherished such visions from day to day, until her residence in London began to become insupportable and tedius to her; and it was with no ordinary satisfaction that she received a summons from Argyle House, requiring her in two days to be prepared to join their north-ward party.

Comments. Both in narrative and descriptive passages sometimes philosophical comments are given. The actions and incidents are related with the observation. The above given paragraph opens with a general observation regarding the hope of a lover that resembles the bean in the nursery tale. Then he relates this observation with Jeanie's fancy.

It is a narration related to the world of imagination; it is a sort of, what is called, stream of consciousness. In such narrations, the incidents should be a logical outcome of the previous incident. It is then connected with the actual incident i.e. summons from Argyle House.

8

How to Improve Your Writing Power-3
(ARGUMENTATION)

Today, arguments in writing and speaking are very important. In most of the departments of life we want others to believe what we believe. So we have to clear the doubts of the listener and erase his preconceived notions if those are contrary to yours. When you write an article you want to convince your readers, when you give an excuse you give a few cogent arguments. When a child pleads for more money he argues and the father refuses to oblige, preferably by giving arguments. A salesman can convince a customer with

arguments; a leader contesting elections will canvass his audience with the help of arguments. So unless a person is argumentative, he may not be a success in life. So argument is an essential part of prose writing and an ingredient of persuasive speech.

What is an argument ?

Any statement which answers "Why or how or what" of an inference is an argument. *For example*, if we say that "science has done harm" it is an opinion or a point of view. But if we say that "science has done harm because it has made our thinking mechanical" it becomes an argument. In the latter sentence we give the reason of what we say in the first part. So an argument is different from an opinion. Sometimes an inference may be supported with the help of the views of a wellknown writer, philosopher or thinker. One must write succinctly because according to Shakespeare 'brevity is the soul of wit.' Similarly an argument may be given with the help of an example in the statement that "democracy will not succeed in India" can be supported by saying "democracy failed in Pakistan under such circumstances." But an argument can be given in different ways.

Methods of giving arguments

As we have seen above, there are various methods of giving arguments. These are

(a) **By giving the cause.** If you give the causes of a particular statement, the sentence becomes an argument. *For example:* if we say that "Literature is a mirror to social life because it is life seen through literary eyes." The truth of such a statement depends, upon the validity of the second part. So the cause given to prove something must be factually correct. *Secondly,* it should be directly connected with the inference. Suppose I say that "Mr. John will stand first because he belongs to a rich family" I am giving an argument which is not connected with the inference. "Standing first" is in no way connected with "richness of a family." *Thirdly,* the

argument must be comprehensive covering as many aspects as possible, otherwise it is not a good argument. *For example:* if we say "that political parties can educate people because people take part in politics" we are not giving a complete argument.

(b) **By giving illustrations.** This type of argument has two advantages (i) such an argument appeals even to a common person. (ii) argument becomes quite lofty and extends its area. Sometimes an illustration itself is an argument. *For example :*

If we want to say that sports are neglected in schools and colleges, we may put it thus. "John's son who is in 10th standard is not allowed to go to the playground because they think that the studies would suffer." In logic it may not be a forceful argument because an insolated illustration may not prove the validity of a statement but in any case it is an argument.

Many a time an illustration from the recognised known facts like science, history, sociology etc. is given. As the nature of the human beings does not undergo any significant change, the pattern of events or human institutions do not change. So our past experience becomes a guide for our future action. That is why an argument has the validity of truth about it. *For example :* "Religious fanaticism cuts at the roots of national unity as it happened in India because of the communal riots." As the illustration gives something true, the conclusion is definitely true. *Another example:* "Man is gregarious by nature so if we keep him alone we are punishing him. Our conclusion in the argument is based on sociological truth."

An illustration has the force of a simile or a metaphor. A simile or metaphor in a poem or poetic prose makes the idea vivid and clear and lends force to the description. Similarly, an illustration adds to the appeal of an argument. When we assume something to be true, we accept the conclusion derived from the statement with an illustration.

(iii) **By giving contrasts**. An illustration supplements the argument but contrasts throws the idea into relief. *For example :* "The English are not gifted artistically. They are not as musical as Italians. Painting and sculpture have never flourished in England as they have in France." The last two sentences do not seem to be arguments but their assumptions have the force of an argument. The sentences give us contrasts whose assumption is as forceful as an argument can be.

(iv) **By quoting authorities.** Sometimes some authorities are quoted to substantiate our point of view. *For example :* if we say that "for the successful working of democracy people have to shoulder many responsibilities because it has a tendency to degenerate. This is just an opinion. If it is supplemented with: Mr. Nehru believed "Eternal vigilance is the price of liberty" we make it a sort of an argument.

Structure of all Argumentative Paragraphs

It is examined from two points of view (i) Mechanical structure (ii) Presentation.

1. Mechanical structure

From the mechanical point of view the essential parts are (1) Inference (2) Supporting arguments (3) Premises.

Inference is the conclusion which we draw. *For example:* our Conclusion may be that "democracy will be successful in India," "The *Supporting arguments* may be (i) The voters are politically enlightened (ii) People are Catholic in their outlook. These are supporting arguments because they answer "Why" of the conclusion. In other words, if we ask "Why will democracy be a success in India"? The two supporting arguments give the reasons.

The *Premises* of these supporting arguments should also answer one of the questions beginning with 'Why", How' 'What' of the argument. *For example:* the premise for the first argument can be "In the last general elections the voting pattern showed political maturity."

In order to widen the scope of the argument, sometimes we give (a) introductory part and/or (b) modifying part. The introductory part is given to introduce the argument. *For example:* for the first argument given above — "The voters are politically enlightened" — introductory part may be "Elections educate the people and the general elections in India have served this purpose well." This is not an argument it is just introduction. (b) *Modifying part* gives some additional information about the argument but in itself it does not contribute to the argument. *For example* for this very argument modifying part may be "Sometimes even politically enlightened people are misled." This does not support the argument, it modifies the argument, it does not contribute to it.

So the mechanical structure of an argument can be graphically represented thus :

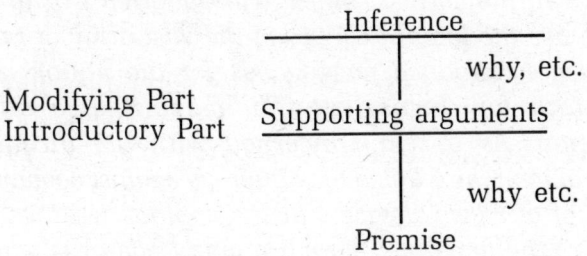

2. Presentation

There are two methods of presenting the arguments
(1) inductive (2) deductive.

In the case of *inductive* method of reasoning, the inference is given at the outset and supporting arguments are given later on.

If we adopt *deductive* method, we give arguments and on the basis of those arguments we come to a conclusion.

Both the methods are equally effective. In both, the writer has to be careful in giving arguments which relate themselves with the inference. The arguments have to be organised in a manner that one leads to the other. Arguments must be interdependent and should not be independent. Thematically disconnected arguments do not allow us to read the passage smoothly.

Examples of Argumentative Paragraphs

PARAGRAPH 1

The policy of planned industrial development which we have adopted in the last two decades has sometimes been criticised as a calculated abandonment of Gandhism. Those who level this charge and advocate cottage industries do not themselves refrain from using the products of large industry such as aircraft, automobiles and telephones. Gandhiji did not shun the railways and was a punctilious user of watches. And if we use railways and watches, does it make sense not to manufacture them ourselves? Gandhi's advocacy of cottage industries should, therefore, be understood in the correct context. He abhorred waste. He wanted to use the latent energies of the vast army of rural unemployed to produce more goods for the nation and some wealth for themselves. Then again, like other sensitization. As a seer concerned with the ultimate condition of man, he wanted to caution us against becoming prisoners of our own devices. In his copious writings on the place of the machine, there are many passages which show that Gandhiji's outlook was broader and more humanely practical than some literalist interpreters would have us believe.

Comments. The first sentence gives a statement which is refuted with the help of arguments. If we analyse the paragraph we can say —

Inference : Planned industrial development which envisages big industries is not unGandhian.

Supporting arguments : (1) Those who advocate cottage industries are using the products of big industries (2) Gandhiji advocated cottage industries because he (a) wanted to use energies of the rural unemployed (b) reacted like a sensitive man to the brutal effects of industrialisation (c) he was humanely practical.

There are modifying parts and introductory parts of many arguments.

As it is a refutation, so the writer has to follow the inductive method of reasoning. He states the inference before he criticises it and disproves it.

PASSAGE 2

There shall be no halting, or half measures, there shall be no compromise or parley. These gangs of bandits have sought to darken the light of the world; have sought to stand between the common people of all the lands and their march forward into their inheritance. They shall themselves be cast into the pit of death and shame, and only when the earth has been cleansed and purged of their crimes and their villainy, shall we turn from the task which they have forced upon us, a task which we were reluctant to undertake, but which we shall now most faithfully and punctiliously discharge. According to my sense of proportion, this is no time to speak of the hopes of the future, or the broader world which lies beyond our struggles and our victory. We have to win that world for our children.

We have to win it by our sacrifices. We have not won it yet. The crisis is upon us. The power of the enemy is immense. If we were in any way to underrate the strength, the resources of the ruthless savagery of that enemy, we should jeopardise, not only our lives, for they will be offered freely, but the cause of human freedom and progress to which we have vowed ourselves and all we have. We cannot for a moment afford to relax. On the contrary we must drive ourselves forward with unrelenting zeal. In this strange, terrible world war there is a place for everyone, man and woman, old and young, hale and hearty; service in a thousand forms is open. There is no room now for the dilettante, the weakling, for the shirker, or the sluggard. The mine, the factory, the dockyard, the salt sea waves, the fields to till, the home, the hospital, the chair of the scientist, the pulpit of the preacher—from the highest to the humblest tasks — all are of equal honour; all have their part to play. The enemies ranged against us, coalesced and combined against us, have asked for total war. Let us make sure they get it.

Comments. The writer follows the deductive method. A large number of the arguments are given to persuade the people to accept the writer's point of view. Its analysis is given below.

Inference : We must wage a total war against the enemy.

Supporting arguments :

(1) Enemy has sought to darken the light of the world.

(2) They are hindering the progress of mankind.

(3) They are criminals, are villains.

(4) Should win war for our children.

(5) If we do not fight, we will risk our life, our freedom and progress.

(6) All are to play some part.

There are a large number of premises, modifying and introductory parts.

PARAGRAPH 3

Smoking is dangerous. The nitrogendioxide in the smoke of a cigarette can produce a solution of acid capable of burning holes in a nylon stocking. And this gas is the agent in cigarette smoke that scientists think may cause emphysema, in which whole clusters of alveoli are gradually destroyed. Only the recovery period between each cigarette and the remarkable mechanism of the lungs and the body enzymes in detoxifying and eliminating poisonous substances show its destructiveness. But Dr. Hurst Hatch flatly declares that any one who regularly smokes two packets a day, will eventually develop emphysema; and may die of it if smoking continues. In prolonged, excessive smoking, the cilia are eventually destroyed. Deposits of tars and volatile condensates in cigarette smoke can then accumulate on the unprotected bronchial surfaces, directly attacking the naked cells. When these cells develop damaged nuclei and become disordered, the result is the first stage of lung cancer.

Comments. The writer has adopted inductive method of reasoning. "Smoking is dangerous" is the inference which is supported with a number of arguments.

9

How to Improve Your Writing Power-4
(INFORMAL WRITING)

I have knowingly dealt with informal writing and omitted formal writing. Formal writings make use of a definite set of words and phrases. If you are writing a memorandum, a note or a draft etc. there is little scope for using your own language. You will have to use stereotyped words and phrases. So, for writing these, one does not need any command over language; the format and language are pre-determined. Under the informal writings fall letters, mostly commercial correspondence, I will exclude from the scope of this chapter because business letters are also stereotyped; there is a great variety in the types but there is little scope for improving the presentation. I will be concentrating on personal letters.

Basic Facts About Letter Writing

ABC of letter writing. A well written letter serves its purpose. In case the letter is not properly organised nor impressively presented, it defeats its aim. So in order to make a letter impressive, we must know what may be called the ABC of a good letter. ABC stands for Accuracy, Brevity and Clarity.

Accuracy is important because the person you are writing to, may not be familiar with the circumstances which caused you to write. So information should be given as accurately as it is possible.

Brevity means that you must pare your letter down to essentials. As a general rule you can organise your letter in three parts—

1. Tell why you are writing
2. Give the important facts
3. Describe what you would like the recipient to do.

The first rule gives the reader what is in your mind, a framework in which to read the letter or a signpost where he is to focus his attention.

The second rule implies that you should give the important facts to support your first sentence. Limit the facts to two, at the most, three. Give reasons in a clear manner — one should be given in one paragraph.

Finally describe what you would like the recipient to do. *For example* if you are complaining to a company, tell them what you want of them.

Clarity is another essential of your letter. There are various methods for doing so (a) keep your paragraphs short (b) keep your sentences short (c) use words which are accurate and simple. Do not use round-about verbiage.

The Mechanics of a Letter

Address and date. If the writing paper is not marked with your address, provide it in the right hand corner of the first page of your letter. Sometimes, specially on a short note, it is given in the lower left hand part of the page just below the level of your signature. *For example*

Sincerely
Jones Mathew

45, Burton Street
Wisconsin

May 5, 20...

Recipient's address. In the case of personal letters there is no need of giving the recipient's address but in business letters or official letters it is necessary. In business letters, the receiver's address should be put at the left, five lines below the level of the date and two lines above the salutation. *For example.*

Smith Johnson and Co.
20, Broadway
New York

The Salutations. For business letters the salutation may be "Dear Sir" or "Dear Sirs". In personal letter, salutation should be selected by keeping the relation one has with the person one writes.

The Beginning. No one is expected to enjoy a letter beginning "I know I ought to have written sooner, but I haven't had anything to write about" or one saying "I suppose you think I have been very neglectful but you know how I hate to write letters". If you merely change the wording of the above-quoted sentences, so that instead of slamming the door in your friend's face you hold it open — "Do you think I have forgotten you entirely ? You do not know, And how many letters I planned to write to you" or "Time and again I've wanted to write to you but each time I was interrupted by something."

It is easy to begin a letter in reply to one you have just received. You have fresh news to comment on, the impulse to reply needs no producing. Nothing can be simpler than to say "We were all so pleased to hear from you this morning," or "Your letter was the most welcome thing the postman has brought for ages." Then you take up the various subjects talked about in the letter before you come to the topics of your own. The beginning should not be abrupt and unimaginative. It is noticed that the candidates begin their letters thus, "In this letter I am going to tell you something about this" or "Thanks for your letter, you have asked me to write about my experiences as a candidate in competitive examination and I am writing." These are the worst type of beginnings in the case of letters. The beginning should be very natural. Lastly, letters in English never begin with a salutation like "good morning" etc.

Ending of a letter. Just as the beginning of a letter should give the reader an impression of greeting, its ending should express friendly or affectionate leave-taking. Nothing can be worse than to flounder for an idea that may affect your escape. Some end their letters with phrase like "Well, I guess you're probably bored by now so I would better close." This type of ending is ungraceful. In personal letters to friends or members of family it is Not necessary to use the standard form of closing like—

Will write again in a day or two

So goodbye for now.

Rest is O. K.

Counting the hours till next weekend

Some Rules of Good Letter Writing

1. Think first of the reader and address yourself to his interests. Tell him all he wants to know and do not leave him to guess between the lines.
2. Adopt a tone suited to the occasion and the purpose of the letter.
3. Write naturally as you would talk, using plain and familiar words.
4. Write clearly and to the point. Avoid round-about and meaningless terms of expression.
5. Write effectively by using simple language, by being consistent and precise.
6. Avoid monotony by repeating ideas or phrases.
7. Pay special attention to opening and closing paragraphs.

MODEL LETTERS

1. *To a friend congratulating him on his brilliant success.*

402, Kavi Nagar
New Delhi

April 25, 20...

Dear Romesh

Your modesty never permitted us to know that you are so brilliant. Your confidence, manner of talking and your interest in studies betrayed your brilliancy. By standing first in this examination is a great achievement. I heartily congratulate you and the members of your family on this achievement. I hope you would host a dinner when you come to this place.

I can easily imagine you working in an important branch of the bank as an officer — the same calm; composed and courteous Romesh who used to meet us in the common room. This career will help your personality to blossom.

But this achievement should not be the end of your ambitions. Work for higher goals; success awaits you at every step. Why don't you come over to me so that we may celebrate your success. Respects to uncle and aunt.

Affectionately yours

Phillip

2. To a friend persuading him to take up the officer's job in the bank instead of joining Allied Services.

21, Nirman Nagar
Kolkata

Jan. 4, 20...

Dear Melvile

God is bountiful and it is for man to make a judicious choice of His bounty. I was surprised to know that you have shown your preference for the Allied Services because, you think, that an officer's job in a bank does not give you authority. But there are many other considerations which must weigh heavily in favour of a job in banks.

The greatest advantage is that you will not be harassed by the politicians. An honest man like you will never be able to comply to the wishes of the politicians. You know the consequences! You will be transferred to some remote area; some charges will be levelled against you. On the other hand, your life in a bank will be smooth and calm. Moreover, as a bank officer you will come in contact with a large number of people. You can oblige many by getting their work done speedily.

So I would like that you should join a bank instead of joining the Allied Services. Respects to uncle and aunt.

Affectionately yours

Richard

3. *To the Commissioner of Police complaining against the anti-social activities of some persons in the campus.*

32, Nehru Nagar
Mumbai

July 7, 20...

The Commissioner of Police
North District
Mumbai

Sir

I want to draw your attention to the anti-social activities of some in the Mumbai University Campus. Some young boys come on motor cycles and cars and drive in the campus very rashly. They would stop their vehicles abruptly in front of the groups of girls. Many girls have been injured. They would pass very indecent remarks. Some of us decided to fight it out with the rowdies. We succeeded in driving them away but only temporarily. They reappeared with some toughs armed with pistols and swords.

We reported the matter to the S.H.O. of the area and for a few days the presence of the police proved effective but afterwards the rowdies became active. Only yesterday they tried to assault a girl. The matter has also been reported to the Vice Chancellor.

I hope you will take personal interest in the matter.

Thanking you

Faithfully yours
John
President
Students Welfare Society

4. *To the editor of a newspaper suggesting ways and means for improving Delhi's Transport Service.*

12, Gandhi Nagar
New Delhi

The Editor
The Statesman
New Delhi

Sir

I shall feel obliged if you publish the following letter in your esteemed daily in the column "Letters to the Editor."

The Lt. Governor of Delhi stressed the need for high capacity transport system at low cost to tackle commuters' problems. The bus transport has definitely proved inadequate; people have to wait for hours together to get a bus. It is almost impossible for the old, the children and the women to board most of the buses. The mini buses and point-to-point running of matadors have added to the difficulties. If more buses are plied, there is a possibility of a larger number of accidents.

Moreover the present traffic network does not cater to the need of the cyclists. They should be provided with fully segregated tracks.

For easing traffic congestion in Delhi, a multi-model system consisting of ring railway and its extensions, buses, light railways and trams in the walled city is perhaps the only answer.

Yours truly
Sydney
(Address)

5. *To the Editor of a Newspaper drawing the attention of the authorities to the need of a library in your area.*

67, Asaf Ali Road
New Delhi
August 5, 20...

The Editor
The Times of India
New Delhi

Sir

Kindly publish the following lines in the column "Letters to the Editor" in your esteemed daily.

Democracy assumes that the voters must be educated so that they can sift the good and bad. This does not imply that one should know the three R's; education is the disciplining of emotions and intellect. Unregulated emotions make us almost animals and indisciplined intellect make us computers. And neither of them is a human being. Education must enlighten the mind and this requires good reading. We must read as much as we can. This is possible only if there are good libraries because no one can afford to spend unlimited amount on books.

In our area, there is no library. During the summer vacations children do not get an opportunity to read. The old have to pass time in gossiping. Our colony has a population of 15000, mostly belonging to the educated class.

So I request the authorities to set up a library as early as possible.

Faithfully yours
Dennis
(Address)

6. *To the manager of a bank complaining against the dishonouring of a cheque.*

The Manager
National Bank Ltd.
Marine Drive
Mumbai

Dear Sir

Vikas Publications Ltd. has informed me that your bank has refused payment of my Cheque No. 527610 of April 25, for Rs. 2000. The returned cheque is marked "Effects not cleared". This, as I understand refers to the cheques which I sent for crediting on 2nd April.

As there has been ample time for you to collect and credit the sums due on the cheques paying in, I shall be glad if you explain why payment of Cheque No. 527610 was refused.

Yours faithfully
George
(Address)

7. Request for loan from a bank without security.

The Manager
The Central Bank of India
Karol Bagh
New Delhi

Dear Sir

In April, 20... you were good enough to grant me a credit of Rs. 5000 which was repaid within the agreed period. I now require a further loan to enable me to proceed with work under a contract with the Delhi Administration for building an extension to some of their school buildings.

I need loan to purchase building material. The contract is for Rs. 75,000 payable immediately upon satisfactory completion of the work on or before 30th Sept. next.

I shall be glad if you grant me a loan of Rs. 60,000 for a period of nine months. The manner in which I have kept my account with you, will justify the loan and since my contract is with a local authority, my ability to pay the loan can hardly be doubted. I am enclosing a copy of my latest audited balance sheet and shall call at the bank at your convenience.

Yours faithfully

Stephen

(Address)

8. To your sister suggesting some interesting books to read.

214, Sector 16 D
Chandigarh

April 14, 20...

My dear Jenny

You must be feeling much relieved after the examination. This type of free time one can enjoy for a day or so only and after that time hangs heavy upon the person. So I think you should read a few interesting books during this period.

I would like you to read A.H. Huxley's book *Brave New World*. It is a novel in which the writer has proved beyond doubt that science alone is neither enough nor desirable. He paints a world where science dominates; children are produced in test tubes and people generally suffer from fits of depression. Ultimately people swing to the religious and the traditional way of living.

Then you should read *Freedom At Midnight* written by the French journalists. It gives a new peep into our struggle for freedom. The style is absorbing and the interesting anecdotes add to the beauty of the book.

I would have sent the books but I think these are easily available at Mumbai. How is Acho ? Respects to mother and father.

Affectionately yours

P Spender

9. Write a letter to your friend regarding the rising prices in India.

Examination Hall

14th June, 20...

Dear John

Your letter has made it quite clear that you have decided not to go to the hill station because of the rising costs. Of course, you are very much justified. Repeated assertions in official circle that the impact of the budget levies on the prices will be nominal has proved wrong. The huge deficit budget has turned the market bullish.

The rise in prices has no relevance to taxes and can be imputed to the desire of the industries to take advantage of the rising demands for goods. By way of illustration, it can be pointed out that even after appreciable fall in prices of cotton, the price of textile goods has increased. It can be said with certainty that there is a conscious and organised effort to create an artificial scarcity to ring up price. But apart from trade and industry, the government must share the blame.

The new excise and levies have raised the prices. Other factors which have contributed it, are rise in money supply, unhealthy growth rate in bank credit, widening trade deficit, liberal imports and declining exports.

With a whopping budget deficit there is bound to be price instability. Then the anticipated record foodgrain harvest, substantial foreign exchange reserves built up over the last two years should give a comfortable feeling. But the area of anxiety is the slow rise in exchange reserves.

The Reserve Bank has launched a two-pronged attack to control credit expansion and keep it within limits. Commercials are told that the increase in credit should be significantly less, both in relative and absolute terms. The cost of credit for big borrowers will be higher than what it was earlier. Past experience shows that the rise in cost of credit does not deter banks from borrowing and reducing lending.

Whatever anti-inflationary measures the government may take, it will have to take into consideration the failure of attempts to role back the price of sugar, gur, textiles, tyres and tractors etc.

Respects to elders.

Faithfully yours

XYZ

10. *Write a letter to your American friend regarding Communalism In India.*

Examination Hall

12th June, 20...

Dear John

Strangely enough you have again fallen a victim to the malicious propaganda carried on by Pakistan against India. Perhaps you know that Hindus and Muslims are two religious communities in India, living together for hundreds of years. It was Mr. Jinnah in conspiracy with the Britishers who sowed the seed of communalism in India. Communal riots in pre-independence India was the exclusive and intolerant character of semitic religion. There are two religious traditions in the world. One Vedic or Indian and the other Semitic. The Vedic tradition to which Buddhism, Jainism, Sikhism and many other smaller sects belong is rooted in the Vedic dictum— God is one, wise men call him by many names. They inspired the Indian concept of respect for all Dharmas. Semitic tradition to which Judaism, Christianity and Islam belong lays stress on particular prophet and books which are mutually exclusive. This is at the root of religious wars among the followers of these religions. During the past two years nearly 2,00000 Christians and Muslims have been killed in similar warfare in Lebanon. More than 50,000 Muslims and Christians have been killed in similar warfare in the Philippines. Similarly religious wars have taken a heavy toll of lives in Nigeria, Chad, Uganda and Sudan.

After partition, about 3 crores of Muslims were left in India. Their number has almost trebled during the last 50 years. As against this, all Hindus and Sikhs have been exterminated or driven out of Pakistan. Things are worse in Bangladesh.

These facts can clearly prove that the Hindus never want to exterminate Muslims. Many a time, the doubtful sincerity of the Muslims lead to trouble. Mutual trust, and faith are necessary. So do not be misled by the Pakistani propaganda against India.

Pay my respects to your mother and father.

Sincerely yours

XYZ

10

How to Increase Your Speaking Power-1
(PERSUASIVE SPEECHES)

A speech differs from other pieces of writings substantially. The main aim of a speaker is (i) to hold the attention of the audience and (ii) to persuade the listeners to believe what the speaker believes. For achieving these aims a speaker has to overcome many hurdles. *Firstly*, his speech should be understandable to the audience. If the audience is educated and well conversant with the subject of the speech, the speaker can make use of technical language without becoming incomprehensible. But if the audience is not well educated the speaker will have to come down to their level. He may have to illustrate points with examples from day to day life. Similarly, if the audience is semi-literate, say students, the speaker may have to adopt the style of a teacher—explaining and illustrating every technical point or term. Clearly, the language of a speech is determined by the audience the speaker is going to address.

Secondly, the language and tone of a speech also depends on the occasion. (i) If the speech is delivered on the death of a person, it should show the intensity of emotions experienced by the speaker. It should arouse similar emotions in the listener's mind. (ii) If the occasion demands that the drooping spirits of the audience is to be boosted, the language will be inspiring, arousing optimism and inculcating hope and aspiration. (iii) If the speaker has instigated the people to rebellion, he will have to use a language which can play with the emotions of the people and can work up their emotions. (iv) If the speech is meant to enunciate a policy or give an exposition of the subject, the style will have to be different.

Thirdly, the language of a speech is also determined by the fact that the audience does not remain attentive all the time. Generally their attention strays away from one point to another unless you are duty bound to listen to it. If you are addressing Press reporters or students on an important topic from the prescribed syllabus, you can expect them to be attentive. But if you are addressing voters or share- holders etc. you cannot assume that they will listen to you attentively. That is why in the speeches some points are repeated. So that you may bring them home to the audience.

Fourthly (i) If you are addressing intellectuals and well educated people, you will have to appeal to their reason. You will have to be persuasive, logical and realistic. But if the audience is prejudiced in favour of the opponent's opinion, you will have to wash off that impression by using words cautiously before your give you own arguments. If you argue out your own point of view without rebutting the opponent's view, your speech will not have the desired effect. If you straight away condemn the opponent's views, perhaps, the audience may not believe you. (ii) If you address just uneducated people, you will have to play upon their emotions. With the help of suggestive words, you make them to feel that

situation demands their action. Sometimes you have to suspend their reasoning power so that they may be swept away from commonly held opinions.

Characteristics of a good speech are given below. All of them taken together determine the style of the speech.

1. **Simple words**. A speech should not have difficult words which may not be understood by the audience.

2. **Simple sentences.** Sentences should not be very long or very short. *Long sentences* cannot be retained in our memory for a long time, so the audience is unable to understand its significance. Clauses in the sentences may distract the attention of the listener. *Short sentences* may go unheard of or unthought of. If they happen to be linking sentences, the whole argument may become useless. If they are introductory sentences, the real context is ignored. But if they happen to be the concluding sentences of an argument they can stick to the listener's mind as slogans.

3. **Logical sequence of ideas.** The ideas contained in a speech should be linked up with the following and previous sentences. The linking up should be thematic and not

otherwise. If sentences are connected with one another with the help of conjunctions, the listener's analytical faculties will have to establish the relationship and it is not possible with a short span of time, which the listener has while listening. So the ideas left by one sentence should be picked by the other thereby weaving a chain.

4. **Elaboration of arguments.** Every argument should be elaborated. It may be done with the help of examples or by analysing the different points of the argument. Examine it from different points of view. *For example* if a speaker is talking about the impact of say, science on society, take its impact on social life, that is customs, religion, family, social relations etc. Then examine its impact on agriculture. Then on economic life in general etc.

5. **No overpadding should be there.** A large number of the arguments should not be given in speech. All good speeches have only a few arguments but those are properly explained, analysed and elaborated. If you use minimum number of words in each sentence, you cannot impress the listener.

Repetition of ideas. In good speeches declamatory language is used. The ideas are repeated. But the wording and presentation should be different each time, otherwise speech becomes monotonous and uninteresting. Declamatory style blows up the idea out of its proportion. That is what a speaker should do.

Reason and emotion. In a speech, there should be a fine balance between reason and emotions. Arguments are meant to persuade and appeal to their emotions for sweeping them off the ground. Both are necessary while you are arguing or you are appealing to the people.

In the following pages we will analyse the speeches of great speakers in order to discover the qualities of the good speeches. We will take up speeches from the different domains and different types in order to achieve this end.

POLITICAL SPEECHES

SPEECH 1 : (Diplomatic Persuasion) :

Here in the thirty third month of the war none of us is weary of the struggle; none of us is calling for any favours from the enemy. If he plays rough we can play rough too. Whatever, we have got to take we will take and we will give it back even in greater measure. When we began this war we were a peaceful and unarmed people. We had striven hard for peace.

We had gone into folly over our desire for peace and the enemy started all primed up and ready to strike. But now as the months go by and the great machine keeps turning and the labour becomes skilled and habituated to its task we are going to the ones who have the modern scientific tackle. It is not now going to be a fight of brave men against men armed. It is going to be a fight on our side of people who have not only the resolve and the cause but who also have the weapons.

We shall go forward together. The road upward is stony. There are upon our journey dark and dangerous valleys through which we have to make and fight our way. But it is sure and certain that if we persevere — and we shall persevere — we shall come through these dark and dangerous valleys into a sunlight broader and more genial and more lasting than mankind has ever known.

(Great war speeches: Winston Churchill)

Comments. It is one of the famous war speeches of Churchill. The Second World War had prolonged; resources were near exhaustion and the morale of the people was quite low. Their patience was taxed. They feared that the future was dark. Under such circumstances it was necessary to boost the morale of the people, to inject moral courage in them and to assure them of success. It cannot be done by boasting and particularly when the facts go against you. How cleverly Churchill achieved these, will be clear from the following analysis.

The opening sentence "none of us is weary... from enemy" is to cure their sagging spirit with a sort of autosuggestion. Then he reasons out the initial defeats by saying that "When we began this war we were a peaceful and unarmed people." He gives hope for the future by saying that the English were now well armed and have determination. But too rosy a picture may seem to be unreal so that he makes the people aware of the difficulties, "The road upward is stony" but tells them that this struggle will lead us to "sunlight broader and more genial......".

There is a logical sequence of ideas—one point leading to other. There is enough elaboration to bring the reader to the conclusion. It is carefully worded to achieve the desired effect.

SPEECH 2 : Psychological persuasion

The elections which we called in 1977 brought in a government consisting of loose alliance of opposition groups. There was neither cohesion nor direction...

Take industry. How could those who had consistently attacked the public sector in favour of private profits, be expected to help basic and heavy industries largely government owned even if a few ministers did claim themselves to be socialists. The slogan which originated in the west "Small and Beautiful" came in handy. Yet there was no evidence besides words of substantial help to the small. The Plan was called a rolling plan. When you tried to grasp it, it rolled away.

In administration, the Janata took systematic but covert steps to weed out persons, with socialist and secular credentials. This was done most assiduously in education and the police services. School books written by modern scholars were replaced with unseemly haste. And the loss of faith in the impartiality and effectiveness of the police that we find in some places today is the direct consequence of the caste and communal consideration introduced at that time.

The Janata and the Lok Sabha boasted of restoring the judiciary to its place of respect. Yet they did not hesitate to harass hundreds of persons on the flimsiest ground or to set up kangroo courts, reminiscent of the market place trials of the Middle Ages.

When we took over, I was stunned at the lethargy, the corruption, the utter lack of any sense of responsibility or of urgency of the larger perspective.

Mrs. Indira Gandhi
Message sent to India League
London on Nov. 11, 1980

Comments. For the first time Congress(I) was routed in elections in 1977. The Janata formed the government but remained in power for a short period. Again Congress was voted to power. The message given is more or less a speech in which Mrs. Indira Gandhi gave a scathing criticism of the people in power.

In the first paragraph she gives a list of bad acts of the previous government. It is one of the methods to disarm a listener. Then she takes up specific examples to substantiate her point of view. She criticises their policies with regard to industrial sector. The implication of this part of the speech is that the Janata Party helped only the big industrialists. This reasoning has an appeal to the people who have become socialist in thinking even though the government has failed to adopt true socialistic pattern of society. This is followed by specific examples of corruption in education and police administration.

The speech has a psychological appeal. It is not an outright condemnation of the opposition party. Such a condemnation will be termed as biased and may not appeal to the people. A politician should try to exploit the weaknesses of the people. He or she should cater to their wishes and their views. The views should be moulded in a manner that may be imperceptible.

SPEECH 3 : Intellectual persuasion

Mr. speaker, Mr. Prime Minister, Your excellencies and friends. I am delighted to be here this evening and inaugurate this organisation, the Institute of Constitutional and Parliamentary Studies.

When our people struggled for freedom they wanted not merely to displace an alien government but the alien method of government by police and prisons. Hereafter they said we shall rule with the authority of the people. That was the idea which we had and we thought parliamentary democracy was the best institution we could devise.

It must be said that parliamentary democracy serves its proper function so long as it listens to the voice of the minority and the voice of the opposition. If you do not listen to the voice of the opposition, fanaticism becomes established as a habit and fanaticism undermines the authority of any democratic institution. Fanatics of race and religion, of pride and hate, these are the people who bring down established institutions, and we must, therefore, try to fight any kind of fanaticism.

The government today takes into account the views of the opposition. Democracy has conducted a war with the united will of the parliament and the people of this country. There was no note of discord or disharmony. In other words the government has the good will of the opposition also.

After all we wish to promote the interests of the people and the speaker has suggested to you a number of things. Integration, consolidation, supremacy of the law, cheap and inexpensive justice — these are all pleasant experiences which we think of we put them down as our ideals. Though we have done a great deal yet we have a long way to go before we can say we have achieved those ideals.

(Radha Krishnan : Speech inaugurating the Institute of Constitutional and Parliamentary Studies Dec 10, 1965.

Comments. The speech has a strong intellectual appeal. There is no example, no illustration, and nothing concrete and comprehensible. The arguments are abstract, primarily meant to create intellectual faith. Every argument takes us forward.

PERSUASIVE PASSAGES

(A) War gives a twofold education. It imposes a great common purpose on a nation, which burns up minor and meaner forces in its consuming flame. And it imposes the attitude and conduct which result from a common purpose. The nation becomes something like a society — a band of companions; in fact it becomes a nation. What lessons can our postwar education learn from the schoolmaster, war? How can we retain in peace these two things which war has temporarily taught us: a great common aim and the spirit of fellowship?

I am proposing a methodical and thorough preparation for an important operation, and the following remarks are not intended to be anything but very elementary first aid. I suggest that there are two main elements of character training and that the work is incomplete if either is neglected; and I ask you to consider whether we take much trouble about either.

The first element is training in social behaviour, a difficult and generally neglected task. Self-centered, self-willed creatures as most of us naturally are, it is our fate to be citizens, members of a community. Men are born to four citizenships : they should be able to live as good members of their family, of their community, of their nation, and of the whole human society. How many of the world's troubles can be traced to a failure in one or other of these citizenships — our never mastering the art of living with others, in the family, in the community, in the nation, in international relations! I have put them in order of ascending difficulty; in the art of living as good members of the human race, men have almost everything to learn.

Comments. The above given passage is more or less expository; ideas are explained in a manner that they have an appeal to the reader. The writer has given a parallel in order to highlight the idea. After giving impact of war on education he comes to the definition of education.

He approaches the problem from the negative point of view also. In other words he tells about the harm done to the society. He suggests, though, does not state, that many troubles of the world can be traced to it.

(B) *I have dwelt at some length on science in order to illustrate the danger of flying to phrases like 'a modern education for modern world' without thinking what they mean. Though the development of science is the most characteristic and in some ways most important feature of our civilization, yet how incompletely it covers life, how much remains outside its sway and range, to how many of our needs and problems, it has nothing to say ! The 'modern world' is only partly modern and the most important things in it existed millennia before Darwin or Faraday or Rutherford. Applied science, technology, new techniques in government and economics, are only the changing dress of a human nature that changes all too little. Each age must learn to wear its peculiar dress and be familiar with its own techniques. But it must not be so fascinated with these as to ignore more permanent things. Show your pupil 'Vanity Fair', since he must live in it; but let him be at least as familiar with the 'Delectable Mountains'. It is the weakness of rich and complicated societies like our own that they tend to live in externals, to concentrate on the techniques of their life. But education, while it must provide for these, can only base itself on them at the expense of neglecting more important things. Such an education will produce mere technicians: by a mere technician I mean a man who understands everything about his job except its ultimate purpose and its place in the order of the universe. They are a very common type.*

Comments. The writer wants to bring the reader to the point that science education can produce only technicians who "understand everything about the job except its ultimate purpose." He brings us to this conclusion with the help of a few arguments (a) much remains outside the way of science (b) rich and complicated societies concentrate on externals only.

The arguments are so beautifully integrated with each other that they seem to be one. These have introductory parts, qualifying statements and premises.

11

How to Increase Your Speaking Power-2
(DISCUSSIONS)

Discussion is an important aspect of our daily life. We may discuss a family matter, an office or a national problem or taking part in a group discussion or appearing at an interview. You need the skill to discuss and use language to impress. If your language is weak you will not be able to convince others even if you have strong arguments to give. In order to become a successful member of a club or a debating society or a member of a committee or an interviewee, you must improve your speaking power.

I will restrict myself to the following types of discussions—

(1) general discussion.

(2) group discussion.

(3) interviews.

General Discussion

By 'general discussion' I do not mean discussion in a bus or discussion among friends or discussion with the members of the family. These discussions do not need any specialised technique; in these discussions you just present your own point of view with regard to a particular topic. In a bus, the other participant may be ill-informed or just a lay man. He

may be speaking on the basis of his own experience and may quote his neighbours. Similarly, among friends and colleagues the discussion is restricted to particular level. So by "general discussion" I mean discussion in a committee or in a meeting of decision-making body.

For such discussions we must (1) gather sufficient information on the topic under discussion (2) analyse the problem (3) consider pros and cons and (4) form an opinion. I will not discuss these because these steps would help to discuss well. I do not deny that these steps, if taken, will help you in speaking on a particular topic; you will have sufficient matter at your disposal. *But in this chapter, we are concerned only with the language part of speaking.*

The language in the case of discussions should be (1) perspicuous (2) to the point (3) precise (4) not pithy (5) simple

Perspicuous. If the other participants cannot understand what you say, the discussion becomes useless. In order to make your language clear, we should not indulge in (a) circumlocution (b) ambiguity (c) long sentences (d) mixing of active and passive voice.

(a) Circumlocution. It means roundabout way of saying something. Mr Micawber in Dicken's novel *David Copperfield* wanted to say : "As you are not familiar with London streets I will tell you the route" he says something like this—

As your peregination in the modern city of Babylon has not been extension, I will instal you in the knowledge of the road to be walked upon. (adapted)

Such circumlocuted sentences should be avoided.

(b) Ambiguity. If your sentences are not ambiguous, you drive your point home. Ambiguity may occur because of various reasons like wrong punctuation, equivocation and telegraphic language. *For example :*

Ambiguous : We were strangers they took us in.

Clear : We were strangers still they took us in.

It is an example of ambiguity due to telegraphic language. We have missed the word STILL and the sentence can be interpreted in many ways.

(c) Long sentences. Some think that very long sentences show one's mastery over the language. But this is wrong. Only those who are not clear in their thinking, speak long sentences. Preferably, there should not be more than two clauses in a sentence. If there are many clauses, the attention of the listener cannot be held.

The sentences should not be very short also. Short sentences may not be listened properly and their significance may be lost. Preferably, a sentence in discussions should consist of two clauses. Both the clauses should be thematically linked with each other.

(d) Active and Passive voice. In active voice, the subject is active whereas in passive voice the subject is passive. A normal person's thinking process conforms with active voice. The idea travels through the verb to the object. By listening or reading, a sentence thinking process is generated. If the

process proceeds smoothly, we understand the meanings easily. So sentences should preferably be in active voice.

To The Point. It means that the speaker should not indulge in (a) digressions and (b) irrelevances.

Rambling sentences which do not focus attention on one point, cannot appeal to the listener. The speaker, moreover, cannot bring the listeners to a definite conclusion. Sometimes, in your zest to score a point you drag the discussion into a domain unrelated to the topic. It is wastage of time and inessential part of discussion. Your arguments should have a direct bearing on the topic. Any argument that does not answer 'why', 'how' or 'what' of the topic, will be irrelevant.

Sometimes we do need some introductory part. Unless we give that part, the argument may seem to be invalid. For example, if we say that "Man needs moral development more than scientific development", we will have to tell a bit about "moral development." It will be introductory but definitely essential for the statement. It will not be irrelevant.

Precise. It means that your language should be exact. This means that the choice of the words should be very judicious. A single loose word may change the meaning of the sentence. It is said that a person was drowning and shouted for help in these words; "I will die, no one shall be able to save me." They say, he was saved but was tried for trying to commit suicide. If you study his words properly, you will find that he has used the verb "will die" which means that he is determined to die. It amounts to trying to commit suicide. He should have used "shall die." So if the language is inaccurate, the purpose of the sentence is lost.

Not Pithy. In discussion, pithy language is out of place because the listener may have to take time to understand its correct meaning. In the case of the written matter, pithy sentences can go but not in the case of discussions. *For example*, if you use Baconian sentences like, "Revenge is a kind of wild justice." We will leave the listeners wondering but not comprehending till you elaborate it. So you can use pithy sentence for beautifying your language but not for furthering your point of view.

Sometimes you have to elaborate and explain the point with the help of illustrations, explanations and analytical approach. All of these methods have already been discussed in this book.

Simple. Simple and racy language is the most effective language. The more clear you are in your thoughts, the more simple you are in your language. Simplicity, we are referring to, is the simplicity of the language which implies that words used by us should be expressive, accurate and not jawbreaking.

Group Discussion

In many competitive examinations like SSB interview, Airlines tests, Public undertaking exams etc. group discussion is a part of interview. The purpose of this is to evaluate whether you can take an initiative in discussions or not, whether you can refute other's arguments, whether you can convince your audience. For achieving these goals, group discussion must include certain essentials. These are :

(1) Language should be elaborative, explanatory and illustrative.

(2) Language should be rhetorical.

HOW TO INCREASE YOUR SPEAKING POWER-2

(3) Language should be simple but effective.

(4) Do not shout at others.

(5) Unnecessary gesticulating should be avoided.

(6) Begin by criticising the argument given by the other speaker and then give your own.

(7) Take the most important point first.

Elaborative, explanatory, illustrative language: In the case of group discussions, the main aim of the speaker should be to drive his point home. Pithy language may make your arguments ineffective and flat. A speaker can emphasise his point by adopting rhetorical or declamatory style. If we say "India has a democratic form of government," it may not be fully grasped by the listener. But if you say "In India, every man or woman who has attained the age of 18, cast their vote to elect their representative. One who bags majority votes in each constituency is elected. The political party which has majority in the Lok Sabha or Legislative Assembly forms the government" you can thrust your point home.

But neither elaboration, nor explanation nor illustration should be too long. If these are unduly lengthened, the main point is lost sight of. In such cases, there is a possibility that another speaker may snatch the initiative from you.

Rhetorical language: Most impressive language for a speech is rhetorical or declamatory. In this type of language we repeat the ideas but not the words. As the audience generally becomes inattentive, unless it is a lecture in a class room, we have to repeat the ideas. Moreover, this is an effective method of emphasising a point. *For example :*

> *Many scores of thousands of troops have been drawn from the immense tropical spaces or from lonely islands nursed by the waves of every sea. Many volunteers were there for whom we could not find arms. Many there are for whom even now we can not find opportunities. But I say that the universal ardour of our colonial Empire to join in this awful conflict, and to continue in that high temper through*

all its ups and downs is the first answer that I would make to those ignorant and envious voices who call into question the greatness of the work we are doing throughout the world and which we shall still continue to do.

The writer in a very clever manner uses mild rhetorical style to bring out the significance of a simple idea. "The colonial Empire have joined hands with the Britishers to fight the enemy." Clearly, it has greater appeal to the listener or the reader.

In this case also, one of the important cautions is that too much of rhetoric will make the style artificial and so unimpressive. *For example :*

Musty, crusty, dusty philosophies
should be abandoned, disowned,
discounted and rejected

The sentence jars upon the ears. It does not make the idea either vivid or appealing. It sounds like changing of bells without rhythm.

Do not shout. While discussing with others one becomes unduly enthusiastic and it is more so in group discussion. The speaker starts shouting at the other participants. This is neither civilised way of discussing nor *correct* method of bringing your point home. Shouts may frighten a servant or a child but not a contestant. Shouting does not leave a wholesome impression on those who are supervising the discussion. Psychologically, only those

(a) who are hollow within i.e. have no convincing argument to give;

(b) who lose their poise suddenly, shout while arguing with others. But sometimes you have to speak a bit louder in order to silence one who tries to side track you for dominating the proceedings.

Reasonable gesticulation. Many speakers wave their hands or head in a menacing manner. Gesticulation is essential for a speaker. Otherwise he becomes a statue speaking something. As in dramas, novels, stories, dramatic performances and paintings, the background scene enhances the effect. In the case of speeches, gesticulation performs this job. It enhances the effect of the stress that you lay on a particular point. A speaker may commit following mistakes in gesticulating—

(1) Gesticulation may be disproportionate to the intended stress. A strong point accompanied by a mild gesticulation or a weak point may be supplemented with wild gesticulation.

(2) Gestures may not be appropriate to the point you are discussing. *For example* a speaker may nod his head while emphasising a point.

Gestures should be used only—

(1) When you have built up the tempo of emotions with the help of words. The audience should reach the crest of emotional wave when you make a forceful gesture.

(2) When the audience seems to be responding favourably to your point of view, gesture at such a point will have the desired effect.

Begin by criticising. In group discussion you must agree or disagree with the previous speaker. It is better to criticise the previous speaker and then give your own point of view. This does not mean that you should always be critical. You may have to speak a second time as your predecessor may have given your point of view. You should have only one point of view and should not contradict yourself.

Most important argument. Give the most important argument in the beginning. Sometimes you start giving weak arguments and the other participant may snatch the initiative. Only a strong argument cannot be so easily rebutted. Group discussion is meant to judge whether a candidate can dominate others and convince them too.

Interview

Interview is different from group discussions in many respects. In the former, you are discussing with your equals and so you become free, frank and informal. But in the case of an interview, you are answering questions to intellectuals who are to judge your performance. So the candidate will have to be formal, respectful and to the point. You cannot digress. Replies should be short and crisp.